Astrological World Cycles
Original First Edition, Copyright 1933

By
Tara Mata (Laurie Pratt)

"Be happy, stay out of debt!"
Yogacharya Oliver Black

From the same publishers:

Dwapara Yuga and Yogananda: blueprint for a New Age
By Poor Richard, 2007

Astrological World Cycles
By Tara Mata (Laurie Pratt)
First published 1932-33 in Yogananda's East-West
Magazine

Copyright 2007 (307 Dwapara)

ISBN: 978-0-6151-8500-2

First Edition

Printed in the United States of America

Table of Contents

Publisher's Preface

The series of articles entitled "Astrological World Cycles" were originally published in Paramhansa[1] Yogananda's East-West Magazine from September 1932 (Volume 4 —11) to October 1933 (Volume 5 —12). At the culmination of the Ananda – SRF Inc. lawsuit in 2002, Yogananda's magazine articles and lessons published before 1943 were declared in the public domain[2]. The text is unchanged from the original, apart from referring to chapters rather than magazine issues, and the addition of some contextual material before the first chapter and after the last.

Any profits from this book will be donated to the One Laptop per Child Foundation (laptopfoundaton.org), which aims to bridge the digital divide in the developing world either directly with its specially created laptops, or in spurring giants such as Microsoft or Intel into action.

---

[1] The Bengali word Paramhansa, meaning "Great Swan", is written Paramahansa in Sanskrit. Yogananda used the Bengali form during his lifetime.

[2] Anandaanswers.com/pages/Who.html

Biographical sketch of Tara Mata

Laurie Virginia Pratt was born on August 16, 1900 in San Francisco. Her life story is intertwined with that of the Indian yogi Paramhansa Yogananda, author of the spiritual classic "Autobiography of a Yogi". In 1924, when she met Yogananda, his welcoming words were "You have come". She joined his organization, SRF Inc.[3], taking the monastic title of Tara Mata.

Tara came from an intellectual family related to Orson Pratt, Joseph Smith, Jr. and Mitt Romney, all of The Church of Jesus Christ of the Latter-day Saints (LDS or Mormons)[4]. Tara's father was a Berkeley Professor. She too was educated there. Tara was a great astrologer, like many of the figures in the following chapters (despite Yogananda's disapproval). She was also close to Edgar Cayce, almost joining his ARE organization[5], where her "life readings" are still on file.

In Tara, Yogananda found a disciple who was both in tune with him and also a strong editor. She notably edited his autobiography and Sri Yukteswar's "The Holy Science", much as her grandfather had edited for Joseph Smith Jr. In her own right, she wrote "Astrological World Cycles" and "A Forerunner of a New Race", the latter recounting her own spiritual experiences.

In 1929, while handling SRF Inc.'s New York operations, she became pregnant and had a daughter, Mona Pratt, who lived for many years near Mount Washington (she is also since deceased). Following the passing of Yogananda and his appointed successor, Saint Lynn, Tara, along with a coterie of LDS converts including Daya Mata, Ananda Mata and Mrinalini Mata, ran SRF Inc.

In 1962, Tara was instrumental in having Swami Kriyananda (J. Donald Walters), then Vice President of SRF Inc. and head of the monastics, expelled[6]. Kriyananda remembers her as eccentric and opinionated

---

[3] Srf-yogananda.org, Non-profit, founded 1920
[4] Lds.org, Non-profit, founded 1820
[5] Edgarcayce.org, Non-Profit, founded 1931
[6] "A place called Ananda" by Swami Kriyananda

but nevertheless a great devotee. She died in Los Angeles, January 18, 1971, two years after a massive stroke. Yogananda said of her:

> "It is not necessary for her to meditate in this life. By editing my writings, and because she came here a highly realized soul, she does not require this. I have already set her place for her in heaven."[7]

Today, SRF Inc. and Ananda[8] are the most well known North American Organizations disseminating the teachings of Yogananda and his Kriya Yoga technique[9]. Tara directly helped in the formation of the first and indirectly inspired the creation of the second. The conflict between the two lead to much of Yogananda's work being in the public domain, beyond the reach of any one organization.

Poor Richard

Texas, USA
December, 307 Dwapara

Dwaparayuga.com

---

[7] SRF Magazine, Summer 1971, "Tara Mata, In Memoriam"
[8] Anada.org, Non-Profit, founded 1968
[9] Please refer to the chapter "Major North American Kriya Yoga Organizations".

Equinoctial World-Age chart

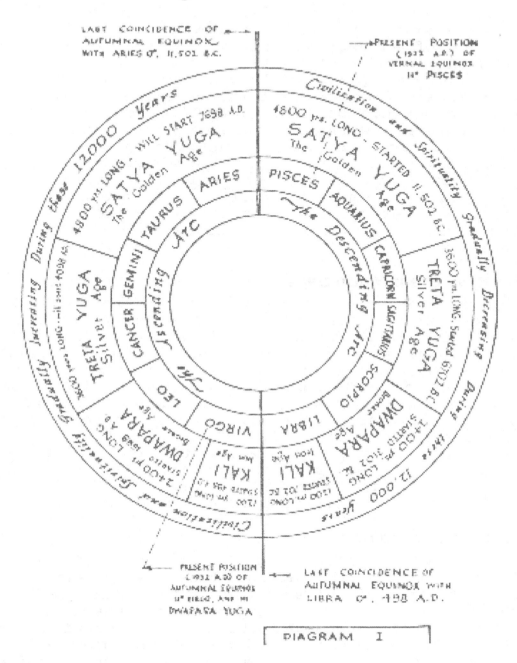

DIAGRAM I

Chapter 1

In a series of articles, of which this is the first, the writer proposes to demonstrate the profound connection of an astronomical phenomenon, known as the Precession of the Equinoxes, with the history of mankind and the great cycles of the world. The true Age, or Yoga, of the present world-period, in reference to the Grand Cycle of Time, symbolized by the stars in their courses, will be pointed out, and certain erroneous ideas that have been circulated by modern philosophical literature, due to misunderstanding of the ancient Hindu Scriptures, will be corrected. The writer will attempt to make all astronomical and astrological references clear enough to be understood by those with only a very elementary knowledge of those sciences.

Authority Is Great Hindu Sage

Readers of this article will be interested to know that the chief authority for the writer's central thesis, which will be developed mainly in the second article of this series, is a small work, published privately in India, entitled: "The Holy Science," by Swami Yogananda's Guru and Master, Swami Sri Yukteswar Giriji Maharaj, founder of Sadhumandal (counsel of sages) and its various Sat-Sanga (fellowship) branches in different parts of India. This saintly Guru is a learned and illuminating commentator on the Bhagavad Gita and other Scriptures, including the Christian Bible, and has, in addition, a grasp of modern science that entitles his views to a very respectful hearing.

Systems of Chronology

The many systems of chronology adopted by different nations at various times are usually the source of great confusion to later historians and archaeologists in their attempts to fix the periods of history. However, whenever the ancients mentioned the position, during their own times, of the planets or of the Equinoxes in reference to the Zodiacal Constellations, the chronological era of such men in world-history can be determined with exactness. An illustration of the truth of this claim, and one which incidentally proves the great astronomical learning of the ancient Egyptians, who could so correctly place the planets, is a mummy's coffin, now in the British Museum, which bears on its cover a Zodiacal representation of the planetary positions at the time the dead Egyptian was embalmed. Calculations by modern astronomers have proved that on the precise date of October 7, 1722, B.C., the planets and luminaries were in the exact positions shown on the coffin design. The mummy can thus be assigned an undeniable antiquity of seventeen centuries before Christ.

All ancient and modern methods of measuring years are based either upon solar or lunar phenomena. Just as a sundial will show the exact time of true noon in any locality, regardless of what system of mean or standard time may be used there, so man has no accurate reference of the passage of time in world cycles through the ages, except the testimony of celestial phenomena.

Precession of the Equinoxes

As every student who goes deeply into the study of any religion, philosophy, or history will find himself confronted with the necessity of understanding the astronomical and even astrological significance of the Precession of the Equinoxes, it is well that this subject be simply and briefly dealt with here.

The equinoctial times are about March 21 and September 22 of each year, when day and night are equal in length all over the earth. This is due to the fact that only on those two days does the earth's axis come to an exact right angle (90°) with an imaginary line running from the center of the Sun to the center of the earth (the equator). The second of time when this right angle is exactly complete, and the Sun is directly in line with the earth's equator, the Sun is considered to have reached the equinoctial points of Aries 0° (the Vernal Equinox, or spring in the northern hemisphere, about March 21) and Libra 0° (the Autumnal Equinox, or fall, in the northern hemisphere, about September 22). The ecliptic, or Sun's annual apparent path around the earth, is measured off, starting with the equinoctial point of Aries 0°, into 360°, 12 signs of 30° each, called the Zodiac of the Signs. This Zodiac, or imaginary belt in the heavens, with the ecliptic as its middle line, is considered to be 16° wide, in order to include the latitude, north and south of the sun's path, of all those planets belonging to our particular solar system. The Sun completes its circuit of this Zodiac of 360° in about 3651/4 days, our solar year.

Zodiac of the Constellations

The Equinoxes having been explained, we shall now consider the meaning of their precession. Modern astronomers have classified every fixed star in the heavens into groups called Constellations. Those groups, however, which lie close to the plane of the ecliptic, were arranged into Constellations in very ancient times, and were considered to form the belt of the natural and actual Zodiac, through which the Sun appeared to travel in its yearly pilgrimage around our earth. This was the Zodiac of the Constellations, and the ancients divided it into 360° or 12 signs of 30° each.

What is the difference between the Zodiac of the Constellations and the Zodiac of the Signs? There is no difference in their division into signs and degrees, or in the astrological influences ascribed to their various parts, but there is, at present, a difference in space between them. There would be no necessity for dual Zodiacs if the Sun, each year, reached its equinoctial point of Aries 0° at exactly the same point of space, measured by reference to some fixed star of the Constellations. However, it has been mathematically determined by astronomers that each year at the moment when the Sun reaches its equinoctial point of Aries 0° and is in exact line with the earth's equator, the position of the earth in reference to some determinant fixed star is some 50" of space father west than the earth was at the same equinoctial moment of the previous year.

The position of any fixed star near the ecliptic and near the borderline of the Constellation Aries could be chosen to be the determinant, or standard reference point, in order to observe this yearly precession of the Vernal Equinoctial Point among the fixed stars. The Hindu astronomers selected Revati as the determinant fixed star, and considered this star as marking Aries 0° of the constellations. Each year the equinoctial point of Aries 0° of the signs will be found to have precessed some 50" of space farther west of Revati than it was the previous year. The meaning of the term, "Precession of the Equinoxes," is now clear. It refers to the slight annual increase in distance of the equinoctial points from a standard fixed star, which is considered as Areis 0° in the Zodiac of the Constellations, while the Vernal Equinox is considered as Aries 0° in the Zodiac of the Signs.

The Central Sun of the Universe

The cause of precession has not been finally established by modern astronomers, some claiming it is due to a slow change in direction of the earth's axis, while others believe they have mathematical proof that the phenomenon is caused by the motion of the Sun in space along its own orbit, whereby all the bodies of our solar system are being brought nearer to a Grand Central Sun, around which our own Sun and every other Sun (fixed star) in the universe is revolving.

All ancient nations considered Alcyone, brightest star of the Pleiades, to be this Grand Central Sun. To the Babylonians it was Temennu, "The Foundation Stone." The Arabs had two names for it—Kimah, the "Immortal Seal or Type," and Al Wasat, "The Central One." It was Amba, "The Mother" of the Hindus, and its present name of Alcyone was derived from a Greek word signifying Peace. It is so far distant from us at present as to appear to be a star of only the third magnitude. There is a significant passage in the Bible (Job 38:4-31) about the Constellation containing Alcyone, where the Lord asked Job: "Where wast thou when I laid the foundations of the earth? Canst thou bind the sweet influences of Pleiades?"

24,000 Years For One Circuit

The great sages of ancient India, whose knowledge of astronomy has not been surpassed by any modern nation, claimed that by the phenomenon of precession the equinoctial points of our Sun would take 24,000 years to complete one circuit around the Zodiac of the Constellations. Modern science tells us that the present rate of precession is 50.1" yearly, or 1°0" in 72 years. At that rate, it would take, not 24,000, but 25,920 years for the Vernal Equinox to make one whole circle of the Zodiac of the Constellations and return to any given starting point (fixed star). However, there is no proof that the present rate of precession, or 50.1" yearly, is constant, and the ancients claimed that at certain stages of the cycle the rate of precession is slightly more rapid than at other stages. This theory receives proof from the calculations of the great astronomer, Hipparchus (146 years B.C.), who gave the rate of precession at the time of his observations as 50-2/3", or a rate somewhat faster than at present. We have, therefore, no scientific reason to deny that the ancient Hindu astronomers were correct in giving

24,000 years as the time, which would elapse between one coincidence of the Vernal Equinox with any fixed star and its next exact coincidence with the same star.

The Four Ages or Yugas

This precessional cycle of 24,000 years is profoundly related to the Four Ages or Yugas into which the ancient rishis (wise men) of India divided each cyclic period. These Ages, known to the Greeks and others as the Golden, Silver, Bronze, and Iron Ages, are as follows:

Satya Yuga —4800 years
Treta Yuga —3600 years
Dwapara Yuga —2400 years
Kali Yuga —1200 years
Total, 12,000 years

It will be seen that two of these cycles of 12,000 equal one complete Precession of the Equinoxes, or 24,000 years, and on this parallel the writer proposes to prove the correct present cyclic Age of the World, and to disprove the current theory that we are still in the dark Iron Age of Kali.

At an important date in Hindu chronology, which would correspond to the year 3102 B.C., the records of Hindu astronomers showed that the last coincidence of the two Zodiacs had occurred 20,400 years previous. As present-day astronomers know that a later coincidence of the two Zodiacs took place in 498 A.D., it will be seen that it required exactly 24,000 years (20,400 + 3,102 + 498 = 24,000), just as the ancients had claimed, for an Equinoctial Precessional Cycle to be completed.

Diagram 1 is very simple, but must be carefully studied in connection with the text.

Daiba Yuga or Electric Cycle

The rishis of old divided the Sidereal Year of 24,000 years, corresponding to the "Great Year" of Plato, into two parts of 12,000 years, each of which embraced a Great Daiba Yuga or Electric Cycle of the Four Ages in the life of mankind and the world generally. One was the Daiba Yuga of the Ascending Arc, and the other of the Descending Arc. The ancients taught that whenever the Sun, in the course of its own revolution, approached most closely to the Grand

Central Sun, Bishnunavi, the seat of Brahma, (this point is reached whenever the Autumnal Equinox, or Libra 0° of the Signs, coincides with the Revati or Aries 0° of the Constellations) the Golden Age of the Descending Arc would begin for mankind.

The Autumnal Equinox was last on Libra 0° in the year 11502 B.C., and the Golden Age of the world (Krita or Satya Yuga) endured from that year until 6702 B.C., or a period of 4,800 years. The ancient calculations tell us that each of the Four Yugas is composed of a main period lasting ten-twelfths of the entire duration of the Age, and of two Sandhis, (mutation or transition periods) one before and one after the main Yuga, each measuring one-twelfth of the total time allowed. Thus, Satya Yuga was assigned a total duration of 4,800 years, consisting of a main period of 4,000 years, which is preceded and followed by Sandhis of 400 years each.

Golden and Silver Ages

The Golden Age of a cycle is the one in which Manu, the great Hindu sage, tells us neither sin nor suffering are common. "Men live four centuries." The ideal length of man's life is limited by the number of years in the Sandhi period of the Age in which he is born.

Treta Yuga, or the Silver Age of mankind, started in 6702 B.C. and continued for 3,600 years, until 3102 B.C. The rule is given in the ancient calculations that, to obtain the length of each of the Yugas after Satya Yuga, the figure one should be deducted from both the number of thousands and of hundreds indicating the duration of each preceding Age and its Sandhis. Hence, the main period of Treta Yuga consists of 3,000 years (one thousand less than that of Satya Yuga), and its two Sandhis are each 300 years long (one hundred less than those of the Golden Age); hence, the total of 3,600 years. During this second Age, men lived for 300 years, and were highly enlightened and spiritually - awakened, though not to such an advanced degree as was reached in the Golden Age.

Bronze and Iron Ages

The year 3102 B.C., a date previously mentioned in the second paragraph of this article, saw the commencement of the Dwapara Yuga of the Descending Arc, the Bronze Age of the ancient world. It lasted until

702 B.C., a period of 2,400 years, which was divided into a main Yuga of 2,000 years, and two transition periods of 200 years each. The traditional account is that the ideal man of that time lived for 200 years. He developed the great ancient civilizations, more concrete and less spiritual than those of the Silver and Golden Ages, but still superior to any civilization of a later growth, all of which come within the limits of the historical epochs of mankind.

The year 702 B.C. saw the start of Kali Yuga, the last of the Four Ages of Daiba Yuga of the Descending Arc. This Iron Age lasted until 498 A.D., or a period of 1,200 years, divided into 1,000 years for the main period of Kali Yuga, and two Sandhis of 100 years each. Most of the ancient world civilizations and empires deteriorated and crumbled away during this period, and by 498 A.D. the creative spirit of mankind was at its lowest ebb. Men did not live beyond a span of 100 years.

This date, 498 A.D., marks the completion of the electric cycle of 12,000 years. Daiba Yuga of the Descending Arc, which is attended by the precession of the Autumnal Equinox from Aires 0° to Libra 0° of the Constellations. The Sun, with its solar system, including our own Earth has traveled, in this period of 12,000 years, from a point in its orbit nearest to the Grand Central Sun to a point farthest away from that seat of universal magnetism, and the history of the world has faithfully portrayed this gradual descent from light to darkness.

An Historical Illustration

H. G. Wells, in his "Outline of History," referring to the condition of mankind about the beginning of the sixth century, A.D. (two years after the close of Kali Yoga of the Descending Arc in 498) says:

"It is not perhaps true to say that the world became miserable in these 'dark ages' to which we have now come; much nearer the truth is to say that the world collapsed into a sea of misery that was already there. Our histories of these times are very imperfect; there were few places where men could write, and little encouragement to write at all. But we know enough to tell that this age was an age not merely of war and robbery, but of famine and pestilence. To many in those

16

dark days it seemed that all learning and all that made life seemly and desirable was perishing."

The Next Golden Age

The year 498 A.D., which saw the Autumnal Equinox on Aries 0°, and the Sun at the nadir of its own orbital path, therefore marks the beginning of the Daiba Yuga of the Ascending Arc, or 12,000 years of gradual progress and improvement, wherein our solar system slowly approaches ever nearer to the Grand Central Sun. This approach will culminate in the year 12498 A.D., when the Autumnal Equinox will reach the fixed star Revati in Aries 0°, and the highest point of our next Golden Age will be attained. Exactly 24,000 years will have elapsed since the previous coincidence, in 11502 B.C. of Libra 0 of the Signs with Aries 0 of the Constellations, and everything in our universe will be in a state of balance and harmony. The year 12498 A.D. will begin a new cycle, a new Daiba Yuga of the Descending Arc, lasting 12,000 years, and thus mankind will descend through a new series of the Four Ages marked out on the Zodiacal Clock of Destiny.

"Such is the great influence of time which governs the universe," writes Swami Sriyukteswarji. "No man can overcome this influence except he, who, blessed with pure love, the heavenly gift of Nature, becomes Divine and, being baptized in the holy stream Pranava (Aum + the sacred vibration), comprehends the kingdom of God."

Returning to a consideration of the last Daiba Yuga of the Ascending Arc, which began in 498 A.D., we find man starting a new Kali Yuga, from which he did not emerge until its period of 1,200 years had passed, in 1698 A.D. Diagram 1 will make it clear that this new Kali Yuga, or Iron (sometimes call Earthen) Age differs from the preceding Kali Yuga of another electric cycle (702 B.C. to 498 A.D.) as the latter was the last Age of Daiba Yuga of the Descending Arc, whereas the Kali Yuga of 498 A.D. to 1698 A.D. is the first age of Daiba Yuga of the Ascending Arc, which is distinguished by a general upward, not downward, trend in history. The seeds sown in the Iron Age of our own cycle are to bear fruit in this our present Dwapara Age.

Age of Our Present Era

The Age of Bronze, or Dwapara Yuga, begun in 1698 A.D., will last for 2,400 years, ending in 4098 A.D.,

2,166 years hence. The present year of 1932 A.D. is thus the year 234 of the Dwapara, or Bronze Age, of the Ascending Arc. At the end of this Age, which is the second of the four ascending Ages (Dwapara Yuga of the Descending Arc is the Third Age.) the intellectual and spiritual power of the average man will be twice as great as that of the ordinary man of 498 A.D. at the beginning of our present 12,000-year cycle, but will be only half as great as the power to be attained by men at the highest peak, 12498 A.D. of the Golden Age of our Daiba Yuga. In other words, the end of our Dwapara Yuga will mark the completion of two of the four ages, and the Divine powers inherent in man will be developed to half their true extent.

The 234th year of Dwapara Yuga corresponds to the present equinoctial positions of Virgo-Pisces 11 degrees. The Vernal Equinox is now falling each spring (in the Northern Hemisphere) among the fixed stars in Pisces 11° of the Constellations, and the Autumnal Equinox is falling among the fixed stars in Virgo 11°. For that reason, mankind is not only in Dwapara Yuga of the cycle of the Four Ages, but is also under the influence of the Virgo-Pisces period of the Cycle of the Constellations.

The signs that lie opposite in the zodiac interact on each other, intermingling their influences to such an extent that it is difficult to separate one form the other. Western astrologers attach most importance to the position of the Vernal Equinox among the constellations, and hence call the present Era the "Piscean Age," but the ancients considered the astrological import of the Autumnal Equinox to be the more significant. We cannot doubt the accuracy of the earlier teachings when we see (diagram 1) that the Vernal Equinox, now falling in Pisces would signify the world as being in the Golden Age, if we grant the spring point primary astrological consequence. None of us are likely to maintain that the present, or the immediate past, history of the world displays the state of near-perfection that belongs to a Golden Age.

World Now in Age of Virgo

On the other hand, the position of the Autumnal Equinox, falling now in Virgo of the Constellations, and in Dwapara Era, does accurately point out the state of present world development, which has lately emerged (in 1698 A.D.) from the historic "Dark Ages" of Kali

Yuga into the greater freedom, intellectual light, and scientific advancement of the Bronze Era. For this reason, we must allow first consideration to the astrological meaning in world-history of the position of the Autumnal, rather than the Vernal, Equinox. Therefore, properly speaking, we are now in the "Age of Virgo," not primarily of Pisces, although Pisces has a very important secondary significance, being indissolubly linked in character and effect with its opposite sign.

Coming Age of Leo-Aquarius

As the equinoxes, at the present stage of their cycle, take 72 years to pass backward through the 60 minutes of space that constitute one degree of the natural or fixed-star Zodiac, and as they are now falling on Virgo-Pisces 11 degrees, it will need about 700 more years before they will coincide with Leo-Aquarius 0°. The coming Leo-Aquarius Age, which will last some 2,000 years, while the equinoxes pass through these opposite signs, will include all the rest of the Dwapara Yuga and part of the third Yuga, Treta, or the immensely enlightened Silver Age.

Next we will point out when and how the mistaken idea and calculation, namely, that the world is still in Kali Yuga, crept into modern Hindu almanacs and astrological and philosophical writings which deal with such subjects as the "Ages" of the world.

Later we will show the fitting application of the term "Bronze Age" to our modern era, and will cite history in demonstration of the sublime correspondence of heavenly phenomena with mundane events.

Chapter 2

The previous chapter dealt with the method used by the ancient Hindu sages to arrive at the correct Age of the world in reference to an astronomical 24,000-year cycle, the Precession of the Equinoxes. Following this plan, we have seen that the present year of 1932, A.D., corresponds to the year 234 of Dwapara Yuga (Bronze Age) of the Ascending Arc. Such a system of chronology commends itself to reason, linking the time-periods of the world with the heavenly phenomena, which alone, by their impersonality, can have an universal significance and application.

Various Chronological Eras

No such universality can be claimed for any other method of chronological reckoning. All systems of national or religious time-keeping have meaning only for a limited group of adherents, and serve as stumbling-stones for historians, since these groups often leave records dated, without explanation, by various chronological calendars, such as civil and religious.

Thus, the year 1932, A.D., of the Christian era, corresponds to the year 5693 of the Jewish era, the year 2592 of the Japanese era, the year 1351 of the Mohammedan era, and the year 2244 of the Grecian (Selecidae) era in present-day usage among the Syrians. Further, of the many chronological eras followed in modern times in various parts of the world, some are reckoned by years based on solar returns, and others on years based on 12 or 13 lunar returns. There is thus room for much confusion among later students of history in their efforts to correctly synchronize past events.

We must grant, therefore, that man can have no more accurate universal measuring-stick for the passage of time than that afforded by the position of the fixed stars in relation to the yearly equinoctial place of the Sun.

Western astronomers, who have not as yet investigated the great universal truths which lie hidden in the ancient division of the 24,000 year Equinoctial Cycle into two sets of four World ages, and who hence, doubtless, would be unwilling to designate the present era as "Dwapara Yuga," would nevertheless be forced to concede that no more practical and accurate method of universal chronology could be adopted than one based on the position of the equinoxes during their 24,000 year cycle.

Reckoning time in this way, we could say, with scientific accuracy, that a new half-cycle (12,000 years) commenced in the year 498, A.D., when the equinoxes coincided with Aries 0° and Libra 0° of the Constellations, and that, as 1,434 years have elapsed since that time, the present year could well be designated in present-day usage all over the world as the "year 1434 since the last coincidence of the two Zodiacs" (or, in more astronomical language, "since the last coincidence of the Vernal Equinox with the fixed star Revati.")

Such a computation would fit in perfectly with the Brahmanical division of the Equinoctial Cycle into World Ages, since, after subtracting 1,200 years, length of the last Kali Yuga, from 1,434, we have a remainder of 234 years, which marks our present place in Dwapara Yuga.

First Error in Calculations

This accurate method of measuring time was current in India for thousands of years, up to about 700, B.C. At that time a colossal mistake crept into the Hindu almanacs and has been blindly perpetrated ever since. Diagram 1 will show that the year 702, B.C., marked the completion of Dwapara Yuga, and the beginning of Kali Yuga, of the Descending Arc.

The Maharajah Judhisthir, who began to reign in India during the latter years of the Dwapara era, voluntarily gave up his throne to his grandson, Raja Parikshit, shortly before the start of Kali Yuga, and retried with all the wise men of his court to a religious retreat in the Himalaya Mountains. Thus, there were none left, at the grandson's court, sufficiently versed in the ancient wisdom, to calculate the Ages correctly.

So, when the last year of the 2,400-year period of Dwapara Yuga passed away, and the first year of the 1,200-year Kali Yuga Dark Age had arrived, the latter was numbered as the year 2401 instead of year 1 of Kali Yuga. In 498, A.D., when the 1,200-year period of Kali Yuga of the Descending Arc had been completed, and the first year of Kali Yuga of the Ascending Arc began, the latter was designated, in the Hindu almanacs, as the year 3601 instead of year 1 of Kali Yuga of the Ascending Arc.

Solar Years Become "Divine" Years

However, as the wise men of that period were well aware, from conditions in India and the world generally, that mankind was in Kali Yuga, the dark Iron Age of Necessity, as described in the prophecies in the Mahabharata, their sacred teachings, and as they also knew that, according to these same scriptures, the age of Kali was fixed at 1,200 years only, they fancied, by way of reconciliation between the scriptures and their current almanacs, that the 1,200 years of Kali were not the ordinary solar year of our earth, but "Divine" years of the gods, consisting of 12 Divine months of 30 Divine days. Each of these Divine days was supposed to be equal in length to one of our solar years.

Thus, the Sanskrit scholars of Kali Yuga, such a Kullu Bhatta, explained away the discrepancies in their almanacs, saying that the 1,200 years allotted by the ancients for the duration of one Kali Yuga were equal (1,200 x 360) to 432,000 solar years of our earth, and that, in 498, A.D., 3,500 years of this long Kali Yuga had passed away. Thus the mistaken calculation gained firmer ground in Hindu chronology, and today the almanacs used in India state that the present year is the 5,034th of Kali Yuga, of which 426,966 years still remain.

Equinoctial Cycle Disregarded

By thus expanding the 1,200 year period into 432,000 solar years, the Kali Yuga teachers entirely lost sight of the connection of the Yugas with the 24,000 year Equinoctial Cycle, and the key to the correct calculation of the World Ages was lost. A modest 24,000-year period is well within the grasp both of the human mind and of historical annals and prehistoric records, but who can hope to trace the characteristic outlines of the two sets of Four Yugas in the affairs of mankind for a period of 8,640,000 years (24,000 x 360)?

No such difficulty faces us if we seek the evidence of the various World Ages in a 24,000 year cycle, and enough is known of the history of mankind for the past 7,000 years (which, rightly, covers our historical period) to enable us to clearly trace the distinctive influence on world events of the various Yugas which have, either completely or partially, run their course during that 7,000 year span.

Mistaken Expansion of Cycle

The erroneous computations of the Four Ages, given out by the Kali Yuga scholars when they discovered their chronology was not in keeping with the rules laid down by the ancient rishis, are as follows:

Satya Yuga, 4,800 X 360 = 1,728,000
Treta Yuga, 3,600 X 360 = 1,296,000
Dwapara Yuga, 2,400 X 360 = 864,000
Kali Yuga, 1,200 X 360 = 432,000
Total Mahayuga in Solar Years, 4,320,000

No justification exists in the Mahabharata, or in the teachings of Manu, for this transformation of solar years into "Divine" years in reference to the Four Ages of the Equinoctial Cycle, yet these mistaken expanded figures have been accepted, without due investigation, not only by the mathematicians who compile the almanacs in present-day India, but also by writers of standard metaphysical and astrological textbooks. These authors have erected, on this shaky mathematical foundation, elaborate cosmological structures which will not stand the test of astronomical verification.

The 12,000-year period, which loses its intrinsic significance when turned into 432,000 years, was known to all ancient civilizations as the half of an Equinoctial Cycle. The old Mazdeans (Magi, of whom the modern Parsis are descendants) had a 12,000-year cycle, Zervan Daregho Hyadata ("Sovereign Time of the Long Period.") With the Greeks and their instructors, the Egyptians, the "Great Age" again referred only to the tropical or sidereal year of the Equinoctial Cycle.

Ancient Atlantean Cycle

There are cycles within cycles—cycles of inconceivably long as well as of unimaginably short duration. It is not, therefore, my aim to contend that the cycle (rather, half-cycle) of 4,320,000 years (Mahayuga or Manvantara) which the Kali Yuga scholars brought into prominence, has no basis in fact. In truth, a solar cycle of that length is recorded in ancient Hindu almanacs as having been preserved from the chronological compilations of a great astronomer-astrologer, Asuramaya, of the old lost continent of Atlantis, but I do wish to point out that, whatever the astrological import of the 4,320,000 year cycle, it should not be confused, as it has been since the dark days of Kali Yuga of the Descending Arc, with the Equinoctial 24,000 year Cycle with its two sets of four World Ages.

Daily 24-Hour Cycle

Our 24-hour solar day, divided (on the equinoctial days) into 12 hours of day (corresponding to Daiba Yuga of the Ascending Arc) and 12 hours of night (corresponding to Daiba Yuga of the Descending Arc), repeats, on a smaller scale, the grand Equinoctial Cycle. According to this plan, the hours of our day would be under the influence of the various Age-vibrations, as follows:

```
Ascending Arc (Day Cycle)
6.00 a.m. to 10.48 a.m. Golden Age Hours
10.48 a.m. to 2.24 p.m. Silver Age Hours
2.24 p.m. to 4.48 p.m. Bronze Age Hours
4.48 p.m. to 6.00 p.m. Iron Age Hours

Descending Arc (Night Cycle)
6.00 p.m. to 7.12 p.m. Iron Age Hours
7.12 p.m. to 9.36 p.m. Bronze Age Hours
9.36 p.m. to 1.12 a.m. Silver Age Hours
1.12 a.m. to 6.00 a.m. Golden Age Hours
```

Daily "Age" Influences

The above arrangement is ideal, rather than practical, since it assumes, for the sake of a simple mathematical division, that sunrise occurs at 6 a.m., and sunset at 6 p.m., whereas this is true only on the equinoctial days, about March 21 and September 22 of each year. This ideal division of a 24-hour day into two 12-hour parts, follows faithfully the Equinoctial Cycle plan of separating the cycle into two divisions of 10 parts each, of which the Kali Yuga period measures one-tenth part, the Dwapara Period two-tenths parts, the Treta period three-tenths parts, and the Satya period four-tenths parts.

Hence, in the compilation given above, the Kali Yuga hour-period measures one-tenth of the 12-hour half-cycle, or one and one-fifth hours, while the Satya Yuga hour-period is as long as four-tenths, or four and one-fifth hours. In practice, however, the length of these hour-periods would vary, according to the season of the year and the latitude of the place on the earth, since all mundane things are under the limitations and changes imposed by time and space.

Daily Zodiacal Hours

Still following the analogy between the 24,000 year Equinoctial Cycle and our 24-hour day, we may (ideally) divide our daily period between sunrise and the following sunrise, into 12 parts of two hours each, and allot the first two hours after sunrise to the influence of the zodiacal Aries, and so on around the circle of the 12 Signs (diagram 1), ending with Pisces ruling the two hours before sunrise of the next day.

The above illustrations may have a more theoretical than practical interest for most of us, since a day is so short that we may not think it worth our while to determine the astrological influences which lie within it, but the examples have been given here in order to point out the relation of smaller to larger cycles, and the mathematical perfection of the Divine Plan which links the greatest to the most infinitesimal within, and doubtless beyond, the shores of our universe.

Chapter 3

Each of the four Yugas, as described by the ancient Hindu sages, has a correspondence with one of the four powers of Maya, the darkness of Illusion that hides from man his Divine nature. Each Yuga brings to mankind in general an opportunity to control and understand one of these universal powers. The four Illusions, Abidyas, of Maya, counting from the grossest to the most subtle, are:
(1) Atomic form, Patra or Anu, the world of gross material manifestation, wherein the One Substance appears as innumerable objects; (2) Space, Desh, whereby the idea of division is produced in the Ever-Indivisible; (3) Time, Kal, whereby the mind conceives of change in the Ever-Unchangeable, and (4) Vibration, Aum, the universal creative force which obscures our realization of the Ever-Uncreated.

This four-fold aspect of Maya is mentioned in the bible in the following passage (Rev. 4:6): "And in the midst of the throne and round about the throne, were four beasts full of eyes before and behind."

Man's Caste in Kali and Dwapara

In Kali Yuga, the knowledge and power of man is confined to the world of gross matter (Bhu Loka, first sphere,) and his state or natural caste is Sudra, a menial or dependent of Nature. During this Yuga, his mind is centered on the problems of material objectivity, the Abidya of Atomic Form.

In Dwapara Yuga, man gains a comprehension of the electrical attributes, the finer forces and more subtle matters of creation. He is then said to belong to the Dwija or twice-born class, since his mind has arisen form the grave of belief in materialism, and he now understands that all matter, atomic form, is in the last analysis nothing but expressions of energy, vibratory force, electrical attributes. During the course of this Age of Dwapara, man is given the power to annihilate the Abidya, Illusion, of Space, and the second limitation of Maya is thereby conquered. During this span, man's mind is centered on the problems of the second sphere of creation (Bhuba Loka) which, by the absence of gross matter and the presence only of Nature's finer electrical matters or energies, is called Shunya, the Vacuum Ordinary.

Man's Powers in Treta Yuga

In Treta Yuga, man extends his knowledge and power over the attributes of universal magnetism, the source of the positive, negative, and neutralizing electricities, and the two poles of creative attraction and repulsion. His natural state or caste in this period is that of Bipra, or perfect (human) class, and he succeeds in piercing the third veil of Maya, the Illusion of Time, which is Change.

The present state of development of human intelligence in this, our own Dwapara Age, is not sufficient to enable us to even dimly understand the problems of the third sphere of Nature (Siva or Swa Loka), that will be met and mastered by the men of Treta Yuga, whose next appearance is scheduled to start in the year 4098 A.D. This third sphere, of universal magnetism, being characterized by the absence of all matter, whether gross or fine, is called Maha Shunya, the Great Vacuum.

In Treta Yuga, the intelligence of man, having penetrated the secrets of the finer material forces of Nature, of Bhuba Loka, in the preceding Age of Dwapara, now comes upon the solution of the mysteries of Swa Loka, the source and origin of all matter-energies, gross and subtle, thus being enabled to comprehend the true nature of the universe. In this state, man's intelligence is sufficiently purified to grasp the principles of Chittwa, universal Heart Atom, magnetic third portion of Creations and throne of Purush, Spirit, the Creator,

The Seven Attributes or "Seals"

Chittwa, the throne, has seven attributes—five kinds of electricities, Panch-Tatwa, the five Root-Causes of creation, and two magnetic poles, one of attraction, Buddhi, the Intelligence which determines what is Truth, and one of repulsion, Manas, the Mind, which produces the ideal world for enjoyment. These seven attributes appear to the spiritual sight as of seven different colors, as in a rainbow. "And there was a rainbow round about the throne." —Rev. 4:3.

The throne of universal magnetism, Chittwa, and its seven attributes, have been compared in the Bible to a sealed casket of knowledge, which no man under Maya, even in Satya Yuga (heaven) can fully understand:

27

"And I saw in the right hand of him that sat on the throne a book written within and on the back side, sealed with seven seals. And I saw a strong angel proclaiming with a loud voice, 'Who is worthy to open the book, and to loose the seals thereof?' And no man in heaven, nor in earth, neither under the earth, was able to open the book, neither to look thereon." —Rev. 5:1-3.

The Fourth Sphere, the "Door"

In Satya Yuga, man comprehends the source of universal magnetism with its principle of duality, or polarity, and his intelligence reaches out to grasp the mystery of Vibration, Aum, the creative power that sustains the universe. "These things saith the Amen (Aum), the faithful and true witness, the beginning of the creation of God." —Rev. 3:14.

If this fourth and last sheath of Maya is thus removed, in the Golden Age, from the eyes of the perfected man, he passes on to the fifth sphere. In this state, freed from the four Illusions, he is called Brahman, knower of the Creator, Brahma, the spiritual light and only Real Substance of the universe. The fourth sphere, Maha Loka, is the connecting link between the three lower Lokas, worlds, and the three spiritual Lokas above, and is thus called Dasamadwar, the Door.

The Seven Spheres or Lokas

The universe, from the Eternal Substance God down to the gross material creation, is divided by the ancient Hindu rishis into seven different spheres, Swargas or Lokas, of which the first four, the kingdom of Maya, have been described above. The remaining three, not being subject to the illusory limitations of vibrations, time, space, or atomic form, are of course unconnected with the time-cycles of the different Yugas, and it will therefore be sufficient here merely to mention them briefly.

The fifth sphere is Jana Loka, the abode of the Songs of God, wherein the idea of the separate existence of the Higher Self originates. As it is above the comprehension of man while under the Illusions of Maya, this sphere is called Alakhsa, the Incomprehensible.

The sixth sphere is Tapa Loka, that of the Holy Spirit or Eternal Patience, as it remains forever undisturbed by any limited idea. Because it is not approachable even by the Songs of God, as such, it is called Agam, the Inaccessible.

The seventh and highest sphere is Satya Loka, abode of God, the only Real Substance, Sat, in the universe. No name can describe it, hence this sphere is called Anam, the Nameless.

"Born of Water and of Spirit"

When man, in Satya Yuga, reaches the fourth, intermediate sphere of Maha Loka, the Door, and overcomes the fourth and last power of Maya, he leaves behind him the illusory world of reflected light, and is baptized directly in the true spiritual light, becoming a son of God. Thus, having been immersed in the sacred stream of Aum (symbolized by water) and illuminated by the direct light of Spirit, he enters into Jana Loka, the Kingdom of God, wherein his own Sonship is made manifest. Jesus answered: "Verily, verily, I say unto thee, except a man be born of water and of the Spirit, he cannot enter into the kingdom of God." —John 3:5.

Thomas saith unto him: "Lord, we know not whither thou goest: and how can we know the way (Door), the Truth, and the Life: no man cometh unto the Father, but by Me." —John 14:5-6. The Door, the fourth sphere of Maha Loka, represents the last Abidya, Illusion, of Maya, which produces the idea of the separate existence of the (lower) self, Ahamkar, Ego, the son of Man. Thus Man, Manava, being the offspring of Maya, Ignorance, and its four powers or illusory ideas, is considered to have his source and origin in these four Ideas or Manus.

The Twenty-Four Tatwa of Creation

The powers of Maya have been divided into twenty-four principles, Tatwa, by the ancient sages, namely, (1) Ahamkar, Ego; (2) Chittwa, Heart Center, universal magnetism; (3) Buddhi, Intelligence; (4) Manas, Mind, (5-19) five kinds of electricities, Pancha-Tatwa, each with three manifestations, and (20-24) Bhoota, five matters of the gross physical world. These twenty-four divisions are mentioned in the Bible as the twenty-four Elders, or primeval principles. "And round about the throne were four and twenty seats: and upon the seats I saw four and twenty Elders." — Rev. 4:4.

The five kinds of electricities manifest in three ways through the three Gunas— Sattwa, the positive, Tama, the negative, and Raja, the neutralizing. The Gunas are the three causative, guiding qualities inherent in and operative upon all Tatwa. The word Guna comes from the roots gu, to work imperceptibly, and nee, to guide. The five positive Sattwa attributes of the electricities are the abstract knowing senses, Jnana-Indriya, through which man realizes his five senses of sight, sound, smell, taste, and touch. Manas, the Mind, guides these Jnana-Indriya through its sense-consciousness.

The five neutralizing Raja attributes of the electricities are the abstract working senses, Karma-Indriya, through which man realizes his five abilities of articulation, motion, generation, absorption, and excretion. The Karma-Indriya are guided by Pran, the Life-Energy.

Five Tanmatra, Subtle Matter
The five negative Tama attributes of the electricities, by their resisting force, produce the five Tanmatra, the objects of the abstract senses. Tanmatra comes from the root, Tat, that, and matra, merely. Tanmatra, then, are Only That or Merely That, the most subtle and most imperceptible form of matter, the vibratory structure of material substance. They are classified as Roop, form and color; Shabda, sound; Gandha, odor; Ras, taste and fluidity; and Sparsha, touch.

These fifteen electrical manifestations, together with the two magnetic poles, Intelligence and Mind, make up the Linga-Sharir or Sukshma-Sharir, the fine material body of Purush, Spirit.

A further increase of the negative Tama Guna, and a combination and mixture of the five Tanmatra, produce the five material substances, or Bhoota, of our physical universe. Bhoota has a root meaning of "to have been." Hence, Bhoota means past. The real nature of the five Bhoota is left behind in time, in their causative Tanmatra, and all the preceding Tatwa. By tracing the etymology of these terms, we realize the great scientific advancement, far out-stripping that of

the scientists of our present era, of the sages who
thus classified the orderly processes of creation.

Chapter 4

The Five Material Bhoota

The first Bhoota is Byoma or Akash, subtle and ethereal fluid that pervades the universe, the peculiar vehicle of light and sound. Its vibration is geometrically represented by a circle enclosing many dots, signifying the atomic movement within limitless space. Akash is subtly connected with the Tanmatra of sound. It is derived from the roots ang, to pervade, and kash, to shine.

The second Bhoota is Wayu. It means "That which flows," from the roots wa, to pervade, and yuk, to augment. It is Wayu that makes aire and all gaseous substances able to manifest. In a subtle sense, it means touch. Its work is expansion, contraction, and pressure. The circular vibration belongs to Wayu. Its form may be seen when a whirlwind causes dust to gyrate in a circular course.

The third Bhoota is Tej, or energy. It comes form the root jejus, light. It causes magnetism, heat, and light. Its work is to expand. In a subtle sense, it is color and form. It causes fire to burn. The triangular rhythm is representative of Tej. and may be observed in the flame of fire, which darts upward in a conical form.

The fourth Bhoota is Apa, or fluidity. It comes from the roots ap, to nourish, and a, partial. Its work is to contract. In a subtle sense, it is taste. It is responsible for all liquids, such as water. Its vibration is semi-circular. The undulating flow of the ocean waves illustrates this rhythm.

The fifth Bhoota is Kshiti or Prithiwi, which gives solidarity. Prithiwi comes from the roots pri, to nourish, th, to stand fixed, and wi, covering. Its work is to harden and make compact. In a subtle sense, it is odor, and in its grossest form, it is earth. It possesses an angular vibration, which causes the composition of matter to be divided into angular particles.

These five Bhoota together make up the gross material body, Sthul Sharir, of Purush, Spirit.

These twenty-four Tatwa, the creative principles of Nature, are described more in detail in a small work, "Cosmic Creation," which was published with the present writer as co-author, in 1922.

These twenty-four Tatwa comprise the whole body of Maya, the illusions of which, separately and collectively, must be known and overcome by man as he progresses through the cycle of the Four-World Ages, and then passes, if his larger individual destiny allows, to the fifth spiritual sphere beyond all mundane conception and cyclic limitation.

Deep Symbolism of "Revelations"

In the following Biblical passages, the four powers of Maya are likened to four beasts; the twenty-four Tatwa or principles of creation, to Elders; the perfected man reborn from the grave of his lower self, to the slain and resurrected Lamb; the seven Spirits of God, to the seven spheres of the universe through which man must pass on his way from selfhood to Godhood; and the mysteries of Nature under Maya, to the Book:

"And I beheld, and, lo, in the midst of the throne and of the four beasts, and in the midst of the elders, stood a Lamb as it had been slain, having seven horns and seven eyes, which are the seven Spirits of God sent forth into all the earth. And he came and took the book out of the right hand of him that sat upon the throne. And when he had taken the book, the four beasts and four and twenty elders fell down before the Lamb." — Rev. 5:6-8.

Procedure for Self-Realization

Rules are given in the masterly little book before referred to—"The Holy Science," by Swami Sri Yukteswarji—for the benefit of the aspirant toward a realization of his own divinity. Such regulations and methods of spiritual achievement as we find in the Bhagavad Gita and other sacred books of India come down to us from an immense antiquity, bearing witness to the Divine knowledge of the ancient sages who could thus guide the chela, disciple, from the darkness of Maya to the light of Spirit through systematic training of body, mind, and soul.

Purification of the material body is enjoined by knowledge of the world of Nature; purification of the electric body by Tapas; religious austerity by moderation or patience both in joy and sorrow, whereby a permanent equilibrium is attained; purification of the magnetic body (Chittwa) by the regulation of the breath as taught by the Guru, whereby one merges himself in the stream of Pranava or Sabda, Aum, the creative vibration.

The Relativity of Yugas

Knowledge of these various steps toward Self-Realization come to man in the natural course of the different Yugas, and the state of mankind in general at any one time determines the Yuga he is living in, or vice versa. However, the Yugas also have their characteristic influence on the individual life cycle of each man, as on each solar day or night, as explained in the last article of this series. Thus, the infancy of man, physically helpless, and mentally undeveloped, corresponds to Kali Yuga, when man is the dependent of Nature. The unfolding powers of reason and the eager idealism of youth is the Dwapara Yuga of the life cycle of an individual, while the ripe powers of maturity are expressed in his Treta Yuga period. Wisdom and compassion, the hard-won gifts of ideal old age, correspond to Satya or the Golden Age of man, about which the poet so beautifully sang:

"Grow old along with me,
The best is yet to be
The last of life,
For which the first was made."

Similarly, the man who has attained freedom, the Jiban Mukta Samnyasi, conqueror of the four Illusions of Maya, is in the Satya Yuga of his own individual cycle, though he may be living in the Kali, Dwapara, or Treta Yuga of the world, and by contrast, appears to be a World Savior by his luminous example. Thus, Jesus, who became a Christ, lived in the Kali Yuga of a world-cycle, but had transcended the fourth sphere, Maha Loka, corresponding to Satya Yuga, and had entered the fifth sphere, Jana Loka, that of the Sons of God.

Chapter 5

We now come to a consideration of the authenticity of this plan of the Four World Ages, in the light of known history and the evidence of pre-history, including that dim stretch of time which begins about 6000 B.C., when the "Dawn of History" appears.

What reason have open-minded students to believe in the truth of this ancient Hindu system of Yuga-chronology, based on the Equinox-Precessional Cycle? Are we really, in our present era, on the Ascending Arc of progress? Has mankind truly emerged, in 1698 A.D., from the Iron Age of Kali into the brighter Bronze Age of Dwapara? Was there actually a Golden Age of the world which ended in 6702 B.C.? Why should we believe in the validity of this Cycle-plan, which conflicts with many others offered in various standard metaphysical and astrological writings, and is unsupported by modern historical interpretation? In short, what are the facts, records and events of the immediate past and of far-distant ages, which can reasonably be admitted as valid evidence of a profound connection between a 24,000 year Equinox-Precessional Cycle of the heavens, and the rise and fall of nations and civilizations on this earth?

In an attempt to answer these questions we must, first of all, consider the orthodox historical view and background, as furnished by our leading anthropologists, geologists, archaeologists, and scholars today.

Beginning of Exact Chronology

H. G. Wells, in his "Outline of History," says, "Chronology only begins to be precise enough to specify the exact year of any event after the establishment of the eras of the First Olympiad (776 B.C.) and the building of Rome (753 B.C.)."

These dates roughly coincide with the beginning of the Dark Age, Kali Yuga of the Descending Arc, in 702 B.C. (It will be necessary for the reader to refer back to diagram 1, in order to properly understand these date-references.)

Thus, we may say that the beginning of history, so far as our modern era has been able to establish an exact chronology is concerned, is coincident with one of the time or Yuga-divisions of the Equinox-Precessional Cycle, whose reliability we shall presently test. The scope of history extends, however, in a far less exact and comprehensive way, to a period about 6000 B.C., which is the date given by modern archaeologists to the Sumerian cities of Nippur and Eridu in Mesopotamia. "Perhaps the earliest people," writes Wells, "to form real cities...In any part of the world, were a people of mysterious origin called the Sumerians...They developed their civilization, their writing, and their shipping, through a period that may be twice as long as the whole period from the Christian era to the present time. The first of all known empires was that founded by the high priest of the god of the Sumerian city of Erech...There flourished the first temples and the first priest-rulers that we know of among mankind."

History Covers Several Yugas

If, then, we take the year 6000 B.C. as marking the "dawn of history," we shall see that this date roughly corresponds to the beginning of the Treta of Silver Age of the Descending Arc, which began in 6702 B.C. In this way, the records of history, starting from the Sumerian empire of a vague 6000 B.C., down to the present day, reveals, completely or partially, the story of mankind for a period of years that would include, by the Age Time-Chart we are using, the entire Yugas of Treta, Dwapara and Kali of the Descending Arc, as well as of the entire Kali and a brief span of Dwapara of the Ascending Arc. Thus, four whole Ages and part of a fifth Age are within the historical period, to whose records we shall presently go in our effort to determine whether or not the distinctive influences of the Yugas can be traced in the life of mankind.

Modern Historical interpretation

Geologists assign to the earth an age of about 1,600,000,000 years. (Einstein, however, has recently stated his estimate as ten billion years.) Anthropologists and other specialists claim that nearly all of that span was without any human life, and put the time of the first appearance of a true human type, the Neanderthal man, at about 50,000 B.C., when the fourth and last Glacial Age was disappearing. By 20,000 B.C., man is represented as having reached, in Egypt and Mesopotamia, the beginning of the agricultural state, the Neolithic or New Stone Age. Finally we

36

arrive, about 6000 B.C., at the "dawn of history" and the first-known cities and civilization of the Sumerians. From then down to the present day, historians claim to discern a more or less steady growth and expansion of civilization and progress among men.

"There are set-backs, massacres, pestilence;" writes Wells, "but the story is, on the whole, one of enlargement. For 4000 years (B.C.) this new thing, civilization...grew as a tree grows; now losing a limb, now stripped by a storm, but always growing and resuming its growth."

This theory of Wells is the theory of nearly all representative modern scholars. Their conception of civilization as a growing tree, first planted, like an acorn-seed of an oak, not earlier than 10,000 B.C., and increasing in stature by slow degrees to the majestic elevation and girth it has now attained, is their primary premise, from which are drawn all their conclusions about the relative importance and height of all civilizations within historical limits. Stated as a syllogism in logic, the argument of historians is this: (1) The path of civilization, seen as a whole, has pursued a straight, upward line through the centuries; (2) The civilizations of ancient Egypt, India, China, Mesopotamia, Cnossus and other centers of early culture, predate modern progress by many thousands of years; (3) Therefore, the ancient world must necessarily have been inferior to those of modern civilization, as represented by the leading nations and greatest minds of our era.

Simple, But Not True

Simple, isn't it? It is also a passably accurate and workable hypothesis, so far as it concerns the evidence of the really well known historical periods, which date, as we have seen, only from the founding of Rome and the beginning of the Kali Yuga of the Descending Arc. Alas, for a theory of such simplicity and one so flattering to the builders of modern culture, "heir to all the ages,"—it is not true. It will not and cannot fit the facts and records of those mighty civilizations which passed through their Golden, Silver and Bronze Ages during the years 11,502 B.C. to 702 B.C.

Civilization, the practical outcome of man's capacity to understand and utilize the powers of knowledge, does not pursue the straight, upward line claimed by historians. Instead, it follows a circular (rather, a spiral) course, with upward and downward half-circles which blend into each other as naturally and inevitably as day follows night, and season succeeds season.

Scholars grant that a cycle of growth and decadence is evident in the history of all past empires and cultures, but they have not yet perceived that the trend of civilization as a whole follows a similar cycle.

"As In Heaven, So On Earth"

The Hermetic axiom, "As above, so below; as in heaven, so on earth," from the Hermetic Law of Correspondences, is the clue. All creation, everything under nature (i.e., Maya), is under a cyclical law. All planets and suns swing around their orbits to complete and resume their individual cycles. The sphere or circle represents perfection of form, and is the archetype of universal structure.

"A philosophy of the history of the human race, worthy of its name," writes Friedrich Ratzel in his History of Mankind, "must begin with the heavens and descend to the earth, must be charged with the conviction that all existence is one — a single conception sustained from beginning to end upon one identical law." Though Ratzel does not perceive the grand implications of his thought, and fails completely to grasp any connection between the heavens and the earth in any sense deeper than the physical realms, yet his words are profoundly true.

Our modern historians and scholars do not understand the universal laws which govern all mundane matters, nor have they yet been able to trace the true and immensely ancient story of civilization during innumerable Equinox-Precessional Cycles or even during one 24,000 year Cycle. Spiritual perception must precede the discovery of truth in even the material worlds, and no human knowledge is ever a certainty until the spiritual law which underlies it is comprehended. To err is human, to know, divine.

"Those who have not practiced devotion conceive erroneously of the nature of the world," runs a passage from the ancient Hindu Puranas. "The ignorant, who do not perceive that this Universe is of the nature of Wisdom, and judge of it as an object of perception only, are lost in the ocean of spiritual darkness.

Viewing civilization as a "new thing" in the story of mankind, and comparing it, as Wells has done, to a tree, starting from an acorn-seed beginning some 6000 or 10,000 years ago and growing steadily, weathering all storms to achieve its present grandeur of size and extent, is a misconception which future historians, in the light of much fuller research and more unfettered minds, will discard.

A 12,000-Year-Old Tree.

It is true, however, that the increase of civilization during the 12,000 years of the Ascending Arc of a complete 24,000 year Equinox-Precessional Cycle, can well be likened to a growing tree. Thus, starting with the year 498 A.D., when the Autumnal Equinox had reached the nadir of its circle and began a climb which will culminate in the year 12,498 A.D., we can discern a slow and gradual improvement of civilization, in comparison with the turmoil and decadence of the world in the preceding 1200 year period of Kali Yuga of the Descending Arc, which lasted from 702 B.C. to 498 A.D.

But the other half of any 24,000 year Equinox-Precessional Cycle, the side represented by the Descending Arc, will never be accompanied by an increase of the general civilization and enlightenment of the world, but will witness the immense spiritual heritage of the Descending Golden Age gradually being lost through the period of the still-glorious Silver Age, and the wonderful material civilizations and achievements of mankind during the Descending Bronze Age being slowly but inexorably broken up and lost during the dark Iron Age. Thus, the last Descending Arc of history measured from 11,502 B.C. to 498 A.D., and the inconceivably high (to our present understanding) Golden Age civilization, which lasted until 6702 B.C., vanished so completely that modern historians will not admit it ever existed. Year by year, during the passage of the Autumnal Equinox down the Descending Arc of it cycle, the knowledge and power of mankind dwindled and perished, until the lowest point of the cycle had been reached, in 498 A.D., and the world was plunged into the near-barbarism that accompanied the fall of Rome and the smash-up of the Western Empire, and the ancient light of India, Egypt and China was nearly extinguished.

The Tree Perishes

If we compare the civilization of the Ascending Arc period to a tree which grows from an acorn-seed to a giant oak in 12,000 years, then we may follow the illustration further and liken the civilization of the Descending Arc to a mighty oak which revolves back to its original state of an acorn-seed, in a manner similar to that shown by a backward exposure of motion picture film. Another comparison would be to a magnificent tree, slowly cut down through the 12,000-year period, its sap drying up and its roots dying in an increasingly barren soil.

Milton, Shakespeare, Solomon

"Time will run back and fetch the age of gold." So wrote Milton, and his use of the words, "run back", is extremely apt, implying both the cycle which links the periods of time to the various Ages, and the retrograde motion of the Autumnal Equinoctial point, against the order of the twelve Zodiacal Constellations.

Shakespeare's works abound in references to the Four Ages of the world. The following passage shows his knowledge of cyclical recurrence (Julius Caesar, 3.1):

"How many ages hence
Shall this our lofty scene be acted o'er.
In states unborn and accents yet unknown."

The imperishable wisdom of Solomon has left us these profound lines (Ecclesiastes 1:9-11):

"The thing that hath been, it is that which shall be; and that which is done is that which shall be done; and there is no new thing under the sun.

"Is there anything whereof it may be said, See, this is new? It hath been already of old time, which was before us.

"There is no remembrance of former things; neither shall there be any remembrance of things that are to come with those that shall come after."

He again says (Eccl. 3:15), "That which hath been is now; and that which is to be hath already been; and God requireth that which is past."

Evolution-Involution cycle

The cyclical law necessitates both evolution and involution, progression and retrogression, regeneration and degeneration. The Sun, sole external life-giver to our planet, wheels around its own orbit, regulating the position of the Autumnal Equinox on the zodiacal path. When the autumnal equinoctial point is falling on the ascending half of its circle of the Zodiac, mankind rises from ignorance to enlightenment, and when it falls on the descending half, the mind of man gradually sinks from illumination to darkness.

This is the law; this is the key to the correct interpretation of the story of mankind through the ages.

This key—an understanding of the connection of the Equinox-Precessional Cycle with the rise and fall of civilizations—has been hidden from the world for over 2400 years, during the course of the two 1200 year periods of the last two Kali Yugas, one of the Descending Arc and one of the Ascending Arc. Now, in our present year of 234 Dwapara Yuga of the Ascending Arc, this knowledge is here being brought to light, for the first time in the Western World, so far as the present writer is aware.

With this key, the historian of some not far distant day in our own Dwapara Yuga will unlock the door which now separates us from a true understanding of the ancient civilizations whose grandeur could, and will instruct and inspire us.

Chapter 6

Modern representative historians, lacking knowledge of the cyclical law which governs the rise and fall of civilizations, and blinded by a fallacious theory that a primitive humanity emerged from a Paleolithic Age and entered a Neolithic or New Stone Age of rudimentary agriculture and the first faint beginnings of human culture about 15,000 B.C., are totally unable to trace the evidences of the glorious civilizations that were actually approaching the full flower of an Ascending Golden Age at that time. Even the more abundant evidence of the civilizations of the Golden and Silver Ages of the last Descending Arc, whose combined periods lasted from 11,502 to 3,102 B.C., has been either misinterpreted or ignored by modern scholars. To understand the folly of their hasty conclusions that the ancient world must have been in a comparatively "backward" stage, it is only necessary to remember that the science of modern Archaeology is still in its infancy.

Archaeological Investigations

"Until the beginning of the 19th century," writes Professor Morris Jastrow, "Egypt, Babylonia and Assyria were little more than names. The spirit of skepticism which accompanies the keen desire for investigation led scholars to question the tales found in classical writers about the great achievements of the Babylonians and Egyptians," and hence gave impetus to actual archaeological research. Egypt, so far, has received the lion's share of archaeological attention, and has yielded, through the Tutankhamen, Gizeh Pyramid and other excavations, enough evidence of the splendor of the Egyptian past to warrant a radical change in modern historical attitude. But India, China, Mongolia, the American continents and other sites of ancient civilizations are still largely unknown and untouched archaeological gold mines. Until they have been explored and excavated for the evidence of their bygone culture, the present dogmatic opinion of the modern historian concerning the role these lands have played in the story of mankind is not only premature but utterly worthless. Future archaeological research in these countries will reveal the unsoundness of the present-day historical views of the past.

The cyclical law in history, whereby the general civilization of mankind rises and falls with the ascent and descent of the Autumnal Equinox on the circle of the Zodiacal Constellations, can shed valuable light on such historical puzzles as the disappearance of the continents and tremendous civilizations of Lemuria and Atlantis. The same Law of Cycles accounts for the lack of continuity in the progress of mankind, and makes it clear why the evidence of the past reveals, at one stage, man in a primitive stage of development, while an earlier stage reveals him as the possessor of mighty arts and sciences far superior to our own. It is the present fashion of scholars to laugh at the idea of cyclical law in history, for to acknowledge its validity would be to destroy their prized theory of a "straight, upward trend of civilization" since the imaginary dawn of a "New Stone Age" about 15,000 B.C.

A Modern View of "Cycles"

"The Indian mind," writes Wells in his Outline of History, "was full of the idea of cyclic recurrence; everything was supposed to come round again. This is a very natural supposition for men to make; so things seem to be until we analyze them. Modern science has made it clear to us that there is no such exact recurrence as we are apt to suppose; every day is by an infinitesimal quantity a little longer than the day before; no generation repeats the previous generation precisely; history never repeats itself; change, we realize, is inexhaustible; all things are eternally new."

With such puerile argument, the historian complacently closes his eyes to the cyclical key which alone is fitted to unlock the door to a true interpretation of history, and to solve the many embarrassing problems, such as Atlantis, with which scholars are at present unable to cope. The law of cyclic recurrence, far from being the "natural supposition" which Wells would make it out, could only dawn in the minds of men with vast trenches of astronomical observation behind them as proof and guide-posts. "Modern science has made it clear to us that there is no such exact recurrence…" —The astronomical constants, like the invariable length of the Sidereal Year and of the absolute daily revolution of the earth on its axis, are apparently not recognized by Wells, especially since he goes on to say, "Every day is by an infinitesimal quantity a little longer than the day before." Evidently he is not aware that about half the days of a year are marked by an increasing shortness in length. Further, he can not even grasp the idea that such cyclic law in an astronomical sense is not from day to day, but from solar year to year, or, in an historical sense, not from "generation to generation," but from Equinoctial Age to Age. "History never repeats itself"—this statement of dogmatic finality is given out by one who admits that the really well-known periods of history start only with the founding of Rome in 753 B.C. but who nevertheless evidently believes himself capable of establishing dogmas on the history of mankind of the last million years.

Though archaeological research has just begun, and has only scraped the surface in a few places in the world, leaving the far greater portion untouched and unknown, and though the evidence of many towering civilizations lie almost inaccessibly hidden under the oceans of the world, yet there is no lack of written and traditional evidence of these ancient cultures. Here again, it is the fashion among present-day scholars to ridicule, misrepresent and misinterpret these venerable sources which, rightly understood, could illuminatingly present the life and knowledge of bygone ages to our modern gaze.

Plato and Herodotus

Thus, Plato's account of Atlantis is treated as historically valueless, and a modern commentator, Jowett, has called it one of Plato's "noble lies." Herodotus, the Greek "father of history" (born 484 B.C.) who visited Persia, Assyria, Babylonia, Egypt and Scythia to study the records of their pasts, wrote an extensive History which is accepted in certain of its parts as authentic fact by modern historians, but rejected as "absurd" and "incredible" wherever Herodotus relates accomplishments of the ancients which modern scholars consider "impossible" of achievement in such early days. Yet every fact given by Herodotus bearing on the high civilizations of ancient lands long past their prime even in his day are being fully confirmed by modern archaeological research. Wells writes: "A wonderful Phoenician sea voyage, long doubted but now supported by some archaeological evidence, is related by Herodotus, who declares that the Pharaoh Necho of the 26th Dynasty commissioned some

44

Phoenicians to attempt the circumnavigation of Africa,"
a trip successfully completed.

Champollion, the peerless French Egyptologist who
was the first to decipher the hieroglyphic symbols,
declared that the "extravagant" tales of Herodotus
about the ancient grandeur of prehistorical Egypt were
no fictions, but that "everything told us by Herodotus
and the Egyptian priests is found to be exact, and is
being corroborated by modern scientists."

Egyptian Chronology

Herodotus and other Greek historians record the
dynastic chronology of the Egyptians as being divided
into four periods—those under the influence of gods,
demi-gods, heroes and mortal men. This four-fold
division likens up clearly with Egyptian history during
the 12,000 years of the last Descending Arc of the
Equinoctial Cycle, and Egypt passed through her Golden,
Silver, Bronze and Iron Ages from 11,502 B.C. to 498
A.D.

Similarly, the esoteric Jewish chronology assigns
Shem, Ham and Hapheth, the three sons of Noah whose
descendants were supposed to have peopled the world
after the great Flood, to a Golden Age, when men lived
for four or more centuries, and places the Babylonian
Captivity in an Iron Age. The Captivity took place
about 586 B.C. or perhaps earlier, but in any case,
near the start (702 B.C.) of Kali Yuga of the
Descending Arc.

Views of French Archaeologists

"Though the origins of ancient Egypt are unknown,
she is found to have been, at the most distant periods
within the reach of historical research, in possession
of her great laws, her established customs, her cities,
her kings and gods; and behind, far behind, these same
epochs we find ruins belonging to other still more
distant and higher periods of civilization. At Thebes,
portions of ruined buildings allow us to recognize
remnants of still anterior structures, the materials of
which had served for the erection of the very edifices
which have now existed for thirty-six centuries!" So
wrote Champollion-Figeac, famous archaeologist and
brother of the Champollion before referred to. These
illustrious French scholars did not, like the majority
of our modern historians, despise the historical facts
contained in such ancient compilations as the Books of

Astrological World Cycles - Original First Edition, Copyright 1933

Hermes, which "truly contain," wrote Champollion-Figeac
in his Ancient Egypt, "a mass of Egyptian traditions
which are constantly corroborated by the most authentic
records and monuments of Egypt of the hoariest
antiquity." He goes on to ask (referring to the
initiated Egyptian priests who were the custodians of
the sacred Hermetic books), "whether there ever was in
the world another association or caste of men which
could equal them in credit, power, learning and
capability?"

Referring to Egyptian temple carvings, an article
entitled What the Old Egyptians Knew, has the following
to say: "Every one of these stones is covered with
hieroglyphics, and the more ancient they are, the more
beautifully we find them chiseled. Does not this
furnish a new proof that history got its first glimpse
of the ancients when the arts were already fast
degenerating among them? That all of these works, in
which solidity rivals the beauty of their execution,
were done before the days of the Exodus, there now
remains no historical doubt whatever." Sir Gardner
Wilkinson adds his testimony, that "he can trace no
primitive mode of life, no barbarous customs, but a
sort of stationary civilization from the most remote
periods."

"The monuments," says Savary in his Letters on
Egypt, "which there strike the traveler, fill his mind
with great ideas. At the sight of the colossuses and
superb obelisks, which seem to surpass the limits of
human nature, he cannot help exclaiming, 'This is the
work of man,' and this sentiment seems to ennoble his
existence."

Pyramids of the Golden Age

"Mechanism," writes Salverte, "was carried by the
ancients to a point of perfection that has never been
attained in modern times Have we not been assailed by
numerous difficulties in striving to place on a
pedestal one of those monoliths that the Egyptians,
forty centuries ago, erected in such numbers?" Many of
the hundreds of pyramids, those "stupendous and
beautiful erections," as Professor Carpenter calls
them, with a "vastness and beauty… still impressive
after the lapse of thousands of years," will be proven
eventually to have been built during the last Golden
Age. Baron Bunsen, one of the best authorities, admits
that "there is nothing improbable in itself in

46

reminiscences and records of great events in Egypt 9000 years B.C." A certain pyramid is described in one of the Books of Hermes as facing the sea, "the waves of which dashed in powerless fury against its base." This passage implies "an origin antedating the upheaval of the Sahara desert."

These colossal structures, which "symbolized the creative principle of Nature, and illustrated also the principles of geometry, mathematics, astrology and astronomy," but which are uncomprehendingly referred to by H. G. Wells as "unmeaning sepulchral piles. Erected in an age when engineering science had scarcely begun," nevertheless present numerous features of engineering skill and technical knowledge unapproached anywhere in our modern world. "The geometrical knowledge of the pyramid-builders," says Professor Smyth, "began where Euclid's ended." Their methods of making imperishable cement and of transporting the huge monoliths from tremendous distances are only two of the many riddles which remain unsolved to this day.

G. R. Gliddon writes, "Philologists, astronomers, chemists, painters, architects, physicians, must return to Egypt to learn the origin of language and writing, of the calendar and solar motion, of the art of cutting granite with a copper chisel, and of giving elasticity to a copper sword, of making glass with the variegated hues of the rainbow, of moving single blocks of polished syenite, 900 tons in weight, for any distance, by land and water, of building arches with masonic precision unsurpassed at the present day, of sculpturing a Doric column 1000 years before the Dorians are known in history, of fresco painting in imperishable colors, of practical knowledge in anatomy, and of time-defying pyramid-building." They also made time-proof papyrus paper, as thin as and tougher than our foolscap paper.

These quotations, and numerous others of similar import, are to be found in Blavatsky's Isis Unveiled, a work which abounds in unassailable evidence of the past glories and knowledge of the ancient world.

H. G. Wells, with his ridiculous assumption that the first civilization and the first known empire of history belong to a mysterious Sumerian people whose beginnings he traces about 6,000 B.C., sees fit to ignore the proven priority of Egyptian civilization, just as he ignores the fact that the almost total absence of archaeological research in India and elsewhere leaves him unfree to draw any sound conclusions or "outline of history" insofar as the story of ancient civilization is concerned. The point cannot be overstressed here, that no proper historical perspective can be gained without a knowledge of the cyclical law which links the Equinoctial Cycle to the periods of growth and decadence among mankind. Only thus can we understand how it is that the highest civilizations of Atlantis, Lemuria, India, Egypt, Assyria, Chaldea, Phoenicia, China, the old Cretan culture of which Cnossus was the center, and the Mongoloid civilizations in ancient Mexico and Peru, so far anterior in time to our present era, were yet superior to any culture of a later growth—just as our own present stage of world development is superior to that which will prevail during the period of the next Kali Yuga of the Descending Arc, from 23, 298 to 24,498 A.D.

Present Stone-Age Men

The discovery of Neolithic remains which appear to date from the periods which our Equinoctial Cycle Age-Chart (diagram 1) would assign to the high ancient civilizations of the last Golden, Silver and Bronze Ages of the descending Arc, is no more indicative of the prevalence of a world-wide primitive stage of development during those periods than the presence of Stone-Age men, such as the Bushmen and Hottentots, the pygmies of the Congo and the natives of Dutch New Guinea and Paupa, in our own present era, can reasonably be said to be representative of world progress today. It is necessary here to repeat that before archaeologists can speak trustworthily on ancient "World-wide" conditions, they must undertake extensive excavations and research work in those lands of ancient culture which have at present received practically no attention. Even Egypt has yielded only a small part of her evidence, and even that belongs mostly to her later and inferior Bronze Age civilization.

Further, archaeologists manifest the most inexcusable reluctance to admit the true dates of their findings, and nearly every date they give for ancient kings and cultures is too close to modern times by several thousands of years. For example, when the Sumerian inscriptions of Sargon I (who founded the

Akkadian empire and conquered the Sumerians during the last Silver Age of the world) were first deciphered, scholars would not grant them an antiquity of more than 1,600 years B.C. It is now generally admitted, by Hilprecht and other authorities, that Sargon I must be assigned of the period around 3,800 B.C., a date which agrees well with the one (3,750 B.C.) given by Nabonidus, last monarch of the Chaldean Empire who flourished about 545 B.C. and conducted antiquarian researches into the history of civilizations past their peak long before his own time.

Chapter 7

The last article in this series threw some light on the antiquity of Egyptian civilization, which Bunsen, the best modern authority, places at 21,000 years B.C., a date he assigns to the erection of the first pyramid. It will be impossible, within the limited scope of this series, to trace in any detail the evidences of the last Golden, Silver and Bronze Age civilizations of India, to study which, as Louis Jacolliet remarks, "is to trace humanity to its sources."

"In the same way," writes this great French scholar, "as modern society jostles antiquity at each step; as our poets have copied Homer and Virgil, Sophocles and Euripides, Plautus and Terence; as our philosophers have drawn inspiration from Socrates, Pythagoras, Plato and Aristotle; as our historians take Titus Livius, Sallust or Tacitus as models; our orators, Demosthenes or Cicero; our physicians study Hippocrates, and our codes transcribe Justinian—so had antiquity's self also an antiquity to study, to imitate and to copy. What more simple and more logical? Do not peoples precede and succeed one another? Does the knowledge, painfully acquired by one nation, confine itself to its own territory, and die with the generation that produced it? Can there be an absurdity in the suggestion that the India of 6000 years ago, brilliant, civilized, overflowing with population, impressed upon Egypt, Persia, Judea, Greece and Rome, a stamp as ineffaceable, impressions as profound, as these last have impressed upon us?"

In another place, Jacolliot says: "The Greek is but the Sanskrit. Phidias and Praxiteles have studied in Asia the chefs d'oeuvre of Daouthia, Ramana and Aryavosta. Plato disappears before Jaimini and Veda-Vyasa, whom he literally copies. Aristotle is thrown into the shade by the Purva-Mimansa and the Uttara-Mimansa, in which one finds all the systems of philosophy which we are now occupied in re-editing, from the Spiritualism of Socrates and his school, the skepticism of Pyrroho, Montaigne and Kant, down to the positivism of Littre."

The Laws of Manu

Jacolliot proves by parallel textual reference (see La Bible de l'Inde, pages 33-47) that the famous

Code of Justinian, Roman basis of modern jurisprudence, was copied from the Laws of Manu, great Hindu legislator whose origin, Jacolliot points out, "is lost in the night of the ante-historical period of India; and no scholar has dared to refuse him the title of the most ancient law-giver in the world."

There is an interesting point which can be made here, in reference to the period of Manu, and the validity of the Equinoctial-World Age plan as presented in these articles. Manu is universally considered in India as having lived during the Golden Age of the world. This assignment is accepted by Sir William Jones, the great Sanskrit scholar, who observes that "many of the laws of Manu are restricted to the first three ages," i.e., a Golden, Silver and Bronze Age. But if the mistaken chronology which has been current in India since about 700 B.C. (as pointed out in the second article of this series) is taken as a basis, we shall see that the last Golden Age of the world ended almost four million years ago. It is manifestly absurd to assign the Laws of Manu to any such remote period. On the other hand, by linking Manu to a Golden Age as determined by the Equinoctial Cycle, we may consider him as belonging to either the last Golden Age of the Ascending Arc, which started in 16,302 B.C., or to the last Golden Age of the Descending Arc, which started in 11,502 B.C.

Another case which verifies the Equinoctial Age-Chart is that of Vyasa, the great expounder of Vedanta, whose date is given in Brahmanical records as 10,400 B.C., and whose works assign him to a Golden Age of the world. We have no difficulty, then, in placing him in the last Equinoctial Golden Age of the Descending Arc.

Hindu Astronomy

Although the scholar Jablonski admits that the Egyptians were familiar for centuries before the historical period with the heliocentric system of the universe, he adds: "This theory Pythagoras took from the Egyptians, who had it from the Brahmans of India." Pythagoras, whose great learning was described by Aristotle, was an Initiate of Egyptian schools, and learned there the truths of the earth's spherical form, the obliquity of the ecliptic, the reflected light of the Moon, the presence of fixed stars in the Milky Way, and other astronomical facts, knowledge of which was subsequently lost to the Western World for the two thousand years of the last two Kali Yugas. All this knowledge is contained in the ancient Hindu Brahmagupta, which points out the fixity of the starry firmament as compared with the dual movement of the earth upon its axis and its yearly circuit around the Sun.

With, then, these few remarks on the enlightenment of India as she passed through the last Golden, Silver and Bronze Ages of her civilization, we shall leave the subject, recommending to the attention of students the scholarly works of Max Muller, Colebrooke, St. Hilaire, Sir William Jones, Weber, Strange, Lassen, Hardy, Burnouf and Louis Jacolliot, all of whom have attempted, with at least some success, to do justice to ancient India. Isis Unveiled, especially Volume I, Section II, by Mme. Blavatsky, is full of well-documented references to the glories of the ancients, and a number of quotations in this article have been culled from its pages.

Records Carved in Stone

Though many of the ancient books have been lost, the majestic ruins of pyramids, labyrinths, caves, palaces and temples, many of them dating from the last Golden Age, still exist, exciting the awe and admiration of all those in the modern world who can read their majestic story aright. "Near Benares," Mme Blavatsky writes, "there are still the relics of cycle-records and of astronomical instruments cut out of solid rock, the everlasting records of Archaic Initiation, called by Sir William Jones old "back records" or reckonings. In Stonehenge (England) they exist to this day. Higgins says that Waltire found the barrows of tumuli surrounding this giant-temple represented accurately the situation and magnitude of the fixed stars, forming a complete orrery or planisphereIn recognizing in the gods of Stonehenge the divinities of Delphos and Babylon, one need feel little surprise." In another place, the same writer says:

"The religious monuments of old, in whatever land or under whatever climate, are the expression of the same identical thoughts, the key to which is in the esoteric doctrine. It would be vain, without studying the latter, to seek to unriddle the mysteries enshrouded for centuries in the temples and ruins of Egypt and Assyria, or those of Central America, British Columbia, and the Nagkon-Wat of Cambodia. If each of these was built by a different nation of whom none had had intercourse with the others for ages, it is also certain that all these structures were planned and built under the direct supervision of the priests. And the clergy of every nation, though practicing rites and ceremonies which may have differed externally, had evidently been initiated into the same traditional mysteries which were taught all over the world. In order to institute a better comparison between the specimens of prehistoric architecture to be found at the most opposite points of the globe, we have but to point to the grandiose Hindu ruins of Ellora in the Dekkan, the Mexican Chichen-Itza in Yucatan, and the still grander ruins of Copan in Honduras. They present such features of resemblance that it seems impossible to escape the conviction that they were built by peoples moved by the same religious ideas, and who had reached an equal level of high civilization in arts and sciences. There is not, perhaps, on the face of the whole globe, a more imposing mass of ruins than Nagkon-Wat, the wonder and puzzle of European archaeologists who venture into Siam." Of these ruins, the French traveler Mouhot says they are "grander than anything left to us by Greece or Rome" and credits their construction to "some ancient Michael Angelos." Frank Vincent confesses the inability of archaeologists to trace their origin. "Nagkon-Wat," he says, "must be ascribed to other than ancient Cambodians. But to whom?"

The Labyrinth of Egypt

Look where one will, the ruins of ancient structures give mute but eloquent testimony that their builders were no primitive Neolithic men, but intellectual and artistic giants. The great Labyrinth of Egypt, already a mass of ruins even in the day of Herodotus, is well described by that historian. He considered it superior to even the pyramids, and as "excelling all other human productions," with its 3000 chambers, half of them subterranean.

Karnak at Thebes is fully as ancient, Champollion, the great French Egyptologist, gives his impressions: "One is astounded and overcome by the grandeur of the sublime remnants, the prodigality and magnificence of workmanship to be seen everywhere. The imagination falls powerless at the foot of the 140 columns of the hypostyle of Karnac!"

The walls of Tiryns, the Cyclopean fortresses of ancient Greece, and the Cyclopean remains of Easter Island, cannot be denied an antiquity less remote than the first pyramids.

Ruins of Ancient Mexico

The origin of the ruins of ancient Mexico and Peru, the palaces and temples of Palenque, Uxmal, Santa Cruz del Quiche, Copan and Arica is so far lost in the mist of time as to give rise to such diverse theories as that (1) they are the work of the ancient Phoenicians, the most enterprising seafaring people of antiquity, whose excursions into the Arctic regions have been chronicled in the Odyssey of Homer, or (2) they were built untold centuries ago by the Atlanteans. Whatever the verdict, it will not be likely to uphold the theory of modern historians who claim, like Wells, that the first civilization started about 6000 B.C. with a mysterious Sumerian people in Mesopotamia.

"Eridu, Lagash, Ur, Uruk, Larsa (Sumerian cities)," writes the historian Winckler, "have already an immemorial past when first they appear in history." The "immemorial past" and civilizations of Egypt, India, China and other countries with less glamour of "mystery" about their origin and achievements than the Sumerians have little interest for the representative modern historian, since he cannot reconcile these facts with his prejudiced misconception that only a primitive Norlithic culture reigned throughout the ante-historical periods.

Ancient Scriptures

The sincere student, then, goes not to the dull and materialistic pages of present-day historians for an understanding of the spiritual wisdom which inspired the ancients and instructed their arts and sciences, but seeks to find the universal message and revelations contained, under diverse allegories, in the sacred scriptures of all the peoples of pre-Kali Yuga antiquity—the Vedas of the Hindus, the Books of Thoth or Hermes of the Egyptians, the Zend-Avesta of Zoroaster, the Kabbalistic Zohar of the Hebrews the Woluspa of the ancient Scandinavians, the Popol Vuh of the ancient Mexicans, the Tanjur of the Tibetans, the mystical Hymns of Orpheus, and the Chaldean Book of Numbers.

The pre-Kali Yuga scriptures, as well as many of the Iron Age, cannot be understood without a key to their symbolism, and to this face may be ascribed the endless colossal blunders which modern scholars have made in translation and interpretation. A literal rendition is often absurd and meaningless, but this fact is the clue that the proper key and insight will yield the most profound knowledge.

Religion intolerance and vandalism were so rampant through the period of the last two Kali Yugas (702 B.B. to 1698 A.D.) that ancient writings, telltale evidence easier to destroy than granite walls and pyramids, were consigned by millions to the flames of fanatical prejudice or artful design.

The Vow of Silence

A third reason for the limited knowledge of the modern world in regard to the depth and extent of bygone civilizations is the strict vow of silence imposed on all Initiates of the Ancient Wisdom, and the necessary caution and ambiguity with which they imparted their great knowledge. The teachings of the Kali Yuga Initiates, such as Pythagoras, a student of the Mysteries or sacred wisdom of Egypt, Babylon, (India, Byblos, Syria and Tyre, and those of Thales, Plato, Lao-Tze of China, Simeon Ben Jochai, the great Hebrew kabbalist, many of the Old Testament prophets, St. Paul, Simon Magus, Apollonius of Tyana, the Essenes' Brotherhood, Marcus Aurelius Antoninus, Plotinus, Proclus, and Paracelsus, all concealed more than they revealed, so that sacred truths might not be profaned nor knowledge of godly powers abused. The two greatest teachers of the last Kali Yuga of the Descending Arc, Buddha and Jesus the Christ, also "spoke in parables."

Thus we have seen, in the facts pointed out in this article, some of the grandeur of the ancient nations of pre-Kali Yuga civilizations, as testified to by the imposing ruins of their stupendous structures, which still embody their knowledge of great arts and sciences, and we have also seen some of the difficulties that face us in our effort to accord a just appreciation to their wisdom and their achievements. With these facts before us, we avoid the delusions of our modern materialistic historians and see the ancients, not as primitive "New Stone Age" men, but as sages and builders enjoying the superior light of intelligence and spiritual perception conferred by the Golden, Silver and Bronze Ages of the Equinoctial Cycle in which they lived.

Chapter 8

The last three articles of this series have mentioned some of the evidence which Egypt, India and other centers of ancient culture have preserved from their last Golden, Silver and Bronze Ages. The year 702 B.C. (diagram 1) marked the start of the equinoctial Kali Yuga or Iron Age of the Descending Arc. This year roughly corresponds to that of the founding of Rome and the start of a history of mankind that can today be recounted with fair chronological accuracy. With these more exact, or more generally accepted and authenticated, records at our disposal, do we find that the fate of empires and the story of mankind have followed a course which can serve as a verification of the Equinoctial Time-Chart we are considering? The answer must be in the affirmative, and the historical record of this 1200-year Iron Age is one of the destruction of proud and mighty empires, of the almost total extinction of the light of human knowledge, and of the prevalence of wars, famines and pestilence. The civilizations and learning of the Golden, Silver and Bronze Ages, gradually diminishing with the passage of the Autumnal Equinox down the Descending Arc of its cycle from 11,502 to 702 B.C., had completely perished by the time the Iron Age came to an end in 498 A.D., and the splendors of the ancient world, overrun by its hordes of barbarian conquerors, were no more.

End of Egyptian Theocracy

Egypt, her Golden and Silver Ages and even the spacious times of her great Bronze Age monarchs, such as Cheops, Amenophis IV and Queen Hatasu, now but a dim memory, fell under Ethiopian rule in 790 B.C., and surrendered the last vestige of her freedom to Alexander in 332 B.C. "Thus," writes J. M. Ragon, "perished that ancient theocracy which showed its crowned priests for so many centuries to Egypt and the whole world." W. J. Colville points out facts which confirm the validity of the Equinoctial Age-Chart, since he says, "One very remarkable fact has impressed all Egyptologists greatly, namely, the vast superiority of the older over the more recent monuments. Egypt apparently has had no infancy or childhood, but appears as though it started on its strange career fully equipped with all the possessions of maturity, and then began at first slowly, then more quickly, to decline."

The same writer has the following to say regarding the Golden Age of the world: "the Greeks, in common with the priests of Egypt, claimed a divine descent, and, from one standpoint at least (the heroic), there is much to substantiate their claims. All nations of antiquity have preserved traditions of a Golden Age in remote antiquity. Though it is always possible to speak of a reputed Golden Age in the past as only a romantic legend pertaining to the infancy of our race, that view by no means suffices to account for the numberless treasures of antiquity being discovered from day to day. The gods of ancient peoples were not altogether mythical or imaginary personages. Their actual history, at least in outline, can be readily traced to remote ages when gods and goddesses were names applied to ruling men and women who were, in a sense, spiritual adepts as well as temporal rulers. To peer no further into antiquity than the period described by the historian, Manetho, we read of the reign of the gods in Egypt continuing in an unbroken line for 13,900 years[10]. These were the Adept-Kings referred to extensively in carefully preserved records now coming under the gaze of general scholars, though for long kept in secret during the Dark Ages of ignorance and persecutions from which we are fast emerging."

Chinese Records "Unsatisfactory"

Egypt was not alone in feeling the weight of Kali Yuga. "Chinese history," H. G. Wells tells us, "is still very little known to European students, and our accounts of the early records are particularly unsatisfactory. About 2700 to 2400 B.C., reigned five emperors, who seem to have been almost incredibly exemplary beings. There follows upon these first five emperors a series of dynasties, of which the accounts become more and more exact and convincing as they become more recent." The Chinese records which are so "unsatisfactory" to Wells, are merely those historical accounts of the high Golden, Silver and Bronze Age civilizations in China, to accept which he would have to discard his elaborate misconceptions about the ancient world. The five "incredibly exemplary" Emperors and the state of the country during their reigns are therefore dismissed without enlargement by Wells, and

---

[10] This span would put the beginning of the line of theocratic rulers back well into the last Golden Age of the Ascending Arc, which endured for 4800 years and ended in 11,502 B.C. Herodotus has the following to say: "The Egyptians assert that from the reign of Hercules to that of Amasis (570 B.C.), 17,000 years elapsed."

he does not breathe freely until the Chinese records touch the Iron Age period, when the accounts become, he says, "more exact and convincing" —that is, more bloodthirsty and ignoble, and thus more in keeping with his own ideas on the nature of the ancients.

The Shang Dynasty, which began in 1750 B.C., and the Chow Dynasty, which rose to power about 1125 B.C., marked the heroic Bronze Age period in China, and even Wells is forced to concede, through the sheer weight of material evidence (which cannot be dismissed as "lies" like mere written records), that "Bronze vessels of these earlier dynasties, beautiful, splendid, and with a distinctive style of their own, still exist, and there can be no doubt of the existence of a high state of culture even (!) before the days of Shang."

With the coming of Kali Yuga, a chaotic state of internal wars and conflict with the invading Huns marked the several centuries which Chinese historians call "the Age of Confusion." A state of profound disorder was manifest under the last theocratic rulers of the Chow dynasty in the 3rd century B.C., and sometime later a part of China's ancient literature vanished under the Emperor Shi Hwang-Ti, who made an attempt to destroy the entire body of the Chinese classics.

Mighty Civilizations Fall

A mighty Aegean civilization disappeared shortly before the start of the Iron Age, with the destruction of Cnossos, and Troy (Hissarlik) by the early Greeks. These ancient sites have recently been excavated. "The Cretan labyrinth was a building as stately, complex and luxurious as any in the ancient world. Among other details we find water pipes, bathrooms, and the like conveniences, such as have hitherto been regarded as the latest refinements of modern life. The pottery, the textile manufactures, the sculpture and painting of these people, their gem and ivory work, their metal and inlaid work, is as admirable as any that mankind has produced. Greek legend has it that it was in Crete that Daedalus attempted to make the first flying machine[11]."

---

[11] Wells admits this much, and also that the Cretan civilization "was already launched upon the sea as early as 4000 B.C.," but he advances some superficial sophistries for the cause of this high culture in such early "Neolithic" days.

The coming of the Dark Age saw the extinction of the Elamite civilization in Mesopotamia. Its chief city, Susa, boasting a culture dating back to the Golden Age, fell to the Persians in the 8th century, C.C. The great Assyrian Empire dwindled away with the fall of Nineveh before the conquering Medes and Persians in 606 B.C. The Chaldean civilization of ancient Babylon perished in the 6th century, B.C. through the devastations of Cyrus and Darius. The bloody career of Alexander "the great" saw the wanton destruction of many cities of great antiquity, including Tyre, Gaza and majestic Thebes, which were razed to the ground and their people sold into slavery. Naught remains today to remind us of Theban glory but the grand ruins of the Golden Age temple of Karnak, which all archaeologists concede could have been built only by men of extraordinary intelligence and artistic gifts.

The older civilization of the Etruscans was wiped out in the 5th century B.C. by the rising Romans and the Gauls from the north. The great days of Greece were over by the 2nd century B.C.[12]; then "gradually barbarism fell like a curtain between the Western civilization and India" (Wells). The early promise of Rome was frustrated by the Punic Wars with ancient Carthage, the "most wasteful and disastrous series of wars that ever darkened the history of mankind" (Wells[13]). The universally famous sea power, Carthage, thus perished by fire at the hands of Rome (146 B.C.) and her population of over half a million people was wiped out. The Greek city of Corinth was murdered by the Romans in the same year.

Caesar "Civilizes" Gaul

Julius Caesar, whose conquest of Gaul is popularly supposed to have "civilized" it, i.e., Romanized it, accomplished nothing more than the destruction of the ancient Kelto-Gaulic civilization. Its chief city,

---

[12] An interesting tie-up with our Equinoctial Age-Chart is found in the periods of the Greek Olympic Games. This institution, dating from the Descending Bronze Age (some authorities give 1453 and others 1222 B.C. as the date of their origin), was discontinued in the 4th century A.D. and not reestablished until 1896 (in Athens), shortly after the start of the Ascending Bronze Age.

[13] Wells is worth quoting here, because his accounts of the well-known historical periods (which start only in the 8th century B.C.) are, generally speaking, as dependable as his accounts of the ante-historical ancients are hopelessly mistaken.

Alesia (now St. Reine), seat of the ancient Gaulic learning and the home of the Druids[14], was plundered and burned by Caesar in 47 B.C. Bibractis (now Autun) in Gaul suffered a similar fate at the hands of the Romans in 21 A.D., and the whole body of her historical and religious literature perished, like that of Alesia, by fire. J. M. Ragon, Belgian authority on Masonic origins, has the following to say:

"Bibractis, the mother of sciences, the soul of the early (European) nations, a town equally famous for its sacred college of Druids, its civilization, its schools, in which 40,000 students were taught philosophy, literature, grammar, jurisprudence, medicine, astrology, occult sciences, architecture, etc., Rival of Thebes, of Memphis, of Athens and of Rome, it possessed an amphitheatre, surrounded with colossal statues, and accommodating 100,000 spectators and in the midst of those sumptuous edifices, the Naumachy, with its vast basin, an incredible construction, a gigantic work wherein floated boats and galleys devoted to naval games; then a Champ de Mars, an aqueduct, fountains, public baths; finally fortifications and walls, the construction of which dated from the heroic ages. A few monuments of glorious antiquity are still there, such as the temples of Janus and of Cybele Arles, founded 2000 years before Christ, was sacked in 270. This metropolis of Gaul, restored forty years later by Constantine, has preserved to this day a few remains of its ancient splendor; amphitheatre, capitol, and obelisk, a block of marble seventeen meters high, a triumphal arch, catacombs, etc. Thus ended Kelto-Gaulic civilization. Caesar, as a barbarian worthy of Rome, had already accomplished the destruction of the ancient Mysteries by the sack of the temples and their initiatory colleges, and by the massacre of the Initiates and the Druids. Remained

---

[14] These Druids, custodians of a high civilization dating at least from the last Silver Age of the world, and builders of the great astronomical structures whose ruins still stand in England (Stonehenge) and in Brittany (Carnac—the ancient European correspondence of the Egyptian Karnak), are mentioned in Isis Unveiled as great "architects, for the immense grandeur of their temples and monuments was such that even now the ruined remains of them 'frighten the mathematical calculations of our modern engineers'," according to a statement in the report of the Archaeological Society of the Antiquaries of London. Further information on the Druids may be found in W. F. Skene's The Four Ancient books of Wales (1868). These Druids are represented by Wells, with his customary perversion of truth in all matters pertaining to the ante-historical ancients, as savages given to human sacrifice!

Rome; but she never had but the lesser Mysteries, shadows of the Secret Sciences. The Great Initiation was extinct."

Rome Meets Her Fate

The 5th century A.D. was Attila and his Huns laying waste to Europe. During the same century, cruel and degenerate Rome met her just fate at the hands of the conquering Goths and Vandals, and the year 493 A.D. (a date practically coincident with the passage of the Autumnal Equinox over the nadir of its cycle) saw Theororic the Ostrogoth on the throne of Rome. "So it was in utter social decay and collapse that the great slave-holding 'world-ascendancy' of the God-Caesars and the rich men of Rome came to an end. We have dwelt on the completeness of that collapse. To any intelligent and public-spirited mind. It must have seemed, indeed, as if the light of civilization was waning and near extinction. The social and economic structure of the Roman Empire was in ruins. It had presented a spectacle of outward splendor and luxurious refinement, but beneath that brave outward show were cruelty, stupidity and stagnation. It had to break down, it had to be removed, before anything better could replace it" (Wells).

The history of the Jews during this Kali Yuga is one far removed from the days of their glory under Saul and Solomon in the Bronze Age. Their Babylonian captivity occurred about 590 B.C. Jerusalem, their sacred city, passed from one alien hand to another, and in 70 A.D., the Roman Emperor Titus completely destroyed the temple and city after a horrible siege.

Palmyra, ancient trading center in the Syrian Desert, fell to the Romans in 272 B.C. and remained a scene of desolate abandonment for centuries thereafter. The great cities of the Anatolian peninsula were all plundered and destroyed by the Persian hordes. By the 6th century, A.D., the ancient magnificent cities of Baalbek (Heliopolis), Amman (Philadelphia) and Gerash, who have left us eloquent evidence of their architectural and engineering skill in Syria, had declined to the state of miserable small towns. The regions of Cilicia and Cappadocia, in eastern Asia Minor, containing many thriving seaport towns thoroughly permeated with a gracious Greek culture, had sunk into barbaric impotency by the end of the 6th century.

India was invaded by barbaric Hunnish hordes during the Dark Age we are considering. The Indo-Scythians founded the Kushan dynasty over all northern India. The Ephthalites came in 470 A.D., and their most powerful leader, Mihiragula, the "Attila of India," inflicted atrocious cruelties upon the people.

So the story goes. There were parts of the world in this Age of Kali which were unaffected (through the action of "cycles within cycles" which provides, according to individual national destiny, for minor Golden, Silver and Bronze Ages within a major Iron Age) by the turmoil and retrogression that marked the affairs of mankind in general during this Dark Yuga. But history gives us the plain story of the correspondence that existed between events on the earth, and the passage in the heavens of the Autumnal Equinox over the lowest part of its cycle. This inauspicious time in the heavens was indeed an inauspicious time upon the earth.

Chapter 9

We now come to a consideration of world history as it followed the rise of the Autumnal Equinox on the Ascending Arc of the Zodiacal circle. The span from 498 to 1698 A.D. comprised the 1200-year period of the Ascending Kali Yuga. We have seen how the last Age (702 B.C. to 498 A.D.) of the Descending Arc was accompanied by the fall of mighty empires and civilizations and the gradual extinguishment of the lamp of knowledge which had so wonderfully illumined the Golden, Silver and Bronze Ages of the ancients. The equinoctial swing from the Descending to the Ascending Arc ushered in new races in new lands; new actors were assigned the leading roles in the historical drama for the new Age. The main scenes shift to new lands: Western Europe, Arabia, Mongolia and America.

A few countries, notably China and India[15], survived the universal wreckage wherein lay the corpses of Egypt, Babylon, Assyria, Sumeria, Crete, Greece and imperial Rome.

Whereas the Ages of the Descending Arc were from greater to lesser, from Golden down to Iron, the Ascending Arc Ages are the reverse, from Iron to Bronze, from Silver to Golden. When the year 498 A.D.[16] introduced the new Iron or Dark Age (Kali Yuga), the first Age of the Ascending Arc, the world broke with the past and started on a new journey of civilization which will culminate in the year 12,498 A.D.

---

[15] The spiritual and cultural roots of India and China were too firmly embedded to be uprooted by the "equinoctial storm" that swept the other great nations of antiquity into oblivion. The destiny of India and China seems, comparatively, timeless; one 24,000 year equinoctial cycle does not see either the beginning or the end of their racial cycles. These cradles of civilization will live to regain all that they have lost during the Dark Ages of the world.

[16] This particular year merely measures to the last exact coincidence of the two (Fixed Star and Equinoctial) Zodiacs. The change from one Age to another is not, of course, confined to the one given year; rather, the change manifests itself not only after but also before a new Age. See the October, 1932, East-West for the length of the transition periods which occur between the Ages, and which combine the influences of those two Ages which they connect.

The Influx of the Nomads

The peoples that spread from the Danube to the Great Wall of China, the nomadic tribes —not barbarians as the historians call them, but certainly without either a settled culture of their own or any practical knowledge of the ancient civilizations that were dying or dead by the time the last hour of the Descending Iron Age had struck—come forcibly into history with the fall of Rome before the conquering Goths and Vandals in the 5th century A.D., though various nomadic tribes had already settled in different European lands during earlier centuries. By the 10th century, the population of Europe differed greatly, racially, from that which had existed during the days of the Roman Empire. Nomadic blood had entered into the people of every European and Asiatic nation. Huns, Goths, Vandals, Alans, Franks, Teutons, Lombards, Czechs, Burgundains, Magyars, Bulgars, Slavs, Norsemen, Ephthalites, Indo-Scythians, Finns, Arabs, Turks, Avars, Angles, Saxons, Jutes, Picts and Scots—all migratory peoples, nomads who had previously wandered between summer and winter pastures in the lands between the Danube and China—had been invading and settling, century by century, in Europe, Africa and Asia. From these races, who intermarried with the peoples whose lands they conquered, our modern races have sprung.

As we are dealing in this article with the influence of the Ascending Equinox on the affairs of the world, we shall trace the gradual betterment of mankind that took place from the fall of Rome to the end (1698 A.D.) of the Ascending Kali Yuga.

The unifying force among the chaotic European states after their conquest by the nomadic peoples was their acceptance of Christianity. By the end of the 11th century, the Pope could appeal with success to the common sympathy of all Europe for the start of the first Crusade. The Age of Feudalism, from the 9th to the 14th centuries, has been called the "Dark Ages" by historians (appropriately enough, from the viewpoint of our Equinoctial time-chart, which places these centuries within the Ascending Dark Age) but feudalism served certain worthy ends in a period of universal insecurity and political confusion. The Crusades had at least two good results: they ended the outworn feudal system, and presented to the European gaze the far more advanced civilization of the Moslem world.

Rise of Mohammedan Arabia

Arabia rose to great power in the 7th and 8th centuries of this Ascending Kali Yuga. Filled with proselyting zeal inspired by their religious leader, Mohammed (570-632), the Arabs conquered and converted peoples from India to Spain, and from the borders of China to northern Egypt. However, their chief contribution to the progress of this Dark Age was the scientific learning which they received mostly through their contact with the decayed but still glorious civilization of India, and which the Arabs disseminated to the Europeans. Many great universities dotted the Moslem world and influenced the later universities of Paris, Oxford and other European centers. The University of Cairo boasted 12,000 students from all parts of the world, so great was the Arab fame for knowledge in mathematics, physics, chemistry, medicine, pharmacy and the use of anesthetics. The introduction of the so-called Arabic numerals, brought from India, was a great stimulation to the European mind. In algebra and spherical trigonometry, the Arabs made great strides; they built astronomical observatories, and produced some of the best astrologers of the time. Their textile fabrics were of marvelous beauty. They followed scientific systems of farming and irrigation, and maintained free schools for the poor. From the Chinese, with whom they traded, came their knowledge of the manufacture of paper and the use of the magnetic needle in navigation. While the monastery schools in Europe were teaching the flatness of the earth, the Arabs were using globes to teach geography. Arabic translations of Aristotle and other Greeks were the introduction of Europe, in the 15th century, to the genius of Grecian thought and literature. Thus it was that the Arabs played a great constructive part in the onward march of progress during this first Age of the Ascending Arc.

Jengis Khan and the Mongols

From the 13th to the 17th centuries, we find a new world power, the Mongol nomads. The amazing empire of Jengis Khan stretched from the Black Sea eastward through China, and from Russia down to northern India. The capital of this vast empire was in Mongolia. The conquests of Alexander, Caesar or Napoleon fade into insignificance when compared with the extent of this Mongol Empire. History tells us much of Mongol ruthlessness, but Jengis was not so wanton a conqueror as Alexander, and the former spared numberless cities and works of art. Complete religious toleration reigned throughout his empire—a boon indeed in a world torn by Christian and Moslem persecutions. The Mongol, courts of Jengis and later of Kublai Khan were the meeting places of all the learned men, merchants and religious representatives of the time. In many ways, the Mongols have played an extremely important role in transmitting and disseminating knowledge. Further, the intermingling of blood that went on between the conquering nomadic Mongols and their subjects, supplied an additional racial diversity to the peoples of the world—a diversity that seems to be a feature of the new Ascending Age, and particularly prominent when we reach the time of the settling of the New World.

"The Travels of Marco Polo," a book dealing with the 13th century experiences of a Venetian adventurer at the court of Kublai Khan, and in China, Japan, Persia, Burma, Sumatra and India as an official and envoy of the Mongol ruler, contributed to a widening of the European viewpoint and interests and was the start of a vigorous intercourse between East and West that proved immensely profitable and instructive to the Europeans, the Mongols also furnished a series of six able rulers in India, of whom Akbar, in the 16th century, was the most beloved. For these reasons, and notwithstanding the barbarous devastations of Hulagu, Timurlane and the Ottoman Turks, we can realize that the Mongols played a major part in furthering the progress of the world during the Ascending Dark Age.

The Progress of Europe

Europe struggled to throw off her chains one by one. The insurrection of the Hussites in Bohemia in 1419 marked the first of the religious wars which finally destroyed the vast temporal power of the Papacy, and released experimental science from ecclesiastical restraint. The widespread Peasant Wars of the 14th century ushered in an era of revolt against social inequality and of claims for the rights of labor that has continued down to our present day. The great revival of learning in Europe started in the 15th century with the introduction of the printing press and paper manufacture. The Renaissance of intellectual vigor which brought the Middle Ages to a close was due to the rediscovery of the old classical culture, the thought of ancient Greece and Rome, of Babylon and Egypt. The distinctive tongues of modern Europe achieved a standard in the 14th and 15th centuries through the literary labors of Dante in Italy, Chaucer and Wycliffe in England, and Luther in Germany, stimulating the growth both of a national spirit and a national literature in the various European countries. The 15th and 16th centuries saw the start of courageous exploration, and the voyages of Columbus to the New World, and the discovery by Vasco da Gama and Magellan of new ocean trade routes to the Orient, resulted in an era of widespread prosperity in Europe.

Names of great thinkers, scientists, writers and artists begin to enter the history of Europe as the Iron Age ascends to its closing centuries. Roger Bacon was the isolated splendor of the 13th century, but the 15th and 15th centuries shone with the genius of Shakespeare, Spenser, Cervantes, Michelangelo, Leonardo da Vinci, Raphael, Francis Bacon and Harvey. Paracelsus was one of the great alchemists, physicians and astrologers of this period. The same centuries produced those pioneer astronomers who laid the foundations of modern astronomical science: Copernicus, Tycho Brahe, Kepler and Galileo.[17] Newton came a century later, and the change, in 1698, from the Iron Age to the Bronze or Dwapara Yuga, occurred during his lifetime.

The 17th century, which brings the Ascending Dark Age to a close, saw a world vastly superior to that of the 5th century, when the momentous climb of the Autumnal Equinox began. The last century of this Kali Yuga witnessed the spread of republican sentiment, with notable results in England, under Cromwell, and in Holland. The same century saw the settling of European colonists in the New World. The stage was admirably set for the next and greater Age (Dwapara) at the start of the 18th century.

Kali Yuga Brings Suffering

That the Kali Yuga of the Ascending Arc, whose history we have been reviewing, was a time of countless woes, of ignorance, wars, plagues and cruel religious intolerance, is beyond dispute. It was an Iron Age, the darkest span of a 12,000-year Equinoctial Arc. Human

---

[17] Biographical histories seldom mention that many of the most eminent founders of modern European astronomy were also devoted students of astrology. Such were Tycho Brahe, Kepler, Newton, Regiomontanus, Flamsteed, first Astronomer Royal of England and the founder of the Greenwich Observatory, and the famous 16th century mathematicians, Jerome Cardan, Lord Napier of Merchiston and Johann Morinus.

misery is the principal theme of the last two Dark
Ages. However, we have seen in the preceding article
that the Kali Yuga of the Descending Arc (702 B.C.-498
A.D.) sank from comparative enlightenment at its start
to social and political chaos and intellectual
stagnation at its end. The Kali Yuga of the Ascending
Arc reversed this sequence. Thus has the Equinoctial
Age time-chart, advocated in this series, proved its
truth and its worth.

Pythagoras and Copernicus

A point of great interest must be mentioned here.
The works of Pythagoras, the Greek philosopher and
scientist who taught the heliocentric theory of the
universe, came to the attention of Copernicus through
the revival of European interest in classical vulture,
and inspired the great Pole to obtain proof of the
truth of the heliocentric theory. Two thousand years
elapsed between the times of Pythagoras (582-507 B.C.)
and Copernicus (1473-1543), and each of these two great
scientists was born a thousand years away from the year
(498 A.D.), which marked the change between the
Descending and Ascending Arcs of the equinoctial cycle.
Because Pythagoras was born in Kali Yuga of the
Descending Arc, he was one of the last teachers in the
ancient western world to maintain the heliocentric
theory, and by the time the Autumnal Equinox had
reached the nadir of its Descending Arc, the false
geocentric theories of Aristotle and Ptolemy had gained
full acceptance. The Equinox traveled a thousand years
on its Ascending Arc before Copernicus arose to revive
the heliocentric theory, and, because he was born in
Kali Yuga of the Ascending Arc, he was one of the first
founders of modern astronomy, and succeeding centuries
saw his work carried on with greater and greater
accuracy and expansion.

In fact, the great age of Hellenic glory—the 6th
and 5th centuries B.C.[18], when Thales, Pythagoras,
Socrates, Plato, Phidias, Pericles, Aeschylus,
Sophocles, Euripides, Meton, Anaxagoras and many other
great intellects produced the last great oasis of
creative culture in the desert of the Descending Dark
Age—has a perfect correspondence in time, according to
our Age-Chart, with the next great intellectual revival
in the western world. The 15th and 16th centuries,

---

[18] These were also the centuries that produced, in the Orient, Guatama, Confucius and
Lao-Tze.

which witnessed the rise of so many stars of learning, are as distant from the nadir, on one side of the equinoctial cycle, as the 6th and 5th centuries B.C. are on the other side. Thus we glimpse—through the connection of the world Ages with the great cycle of equinoctial precession—the measured epochs of our history, and the repetition of opportunity that occurs at equidistant points in that cycle.

Chapter 10

The last article of this series dealt with the slow progress of the last Dark Age, Kali Yuga of the Ascending Arc, which ended at the close of the 17th century (1698 A.D.). A consideration of the next Age, marked out by the gradual rise of the Autumnal Equinox on the zodiacal circle, brings us to our modern era, Dwapara Yuga or the Bronze Age of the Ascending Arc, which will complete its 2400 year period in 4098 A.D.

Our present year, 1933 A.D., is the 235th year of Dwapara Yuga, and world progress has made greater strides in those two and one-third centuries than in all the twenty-four centuries (comprising two Kali Yugas) that preceded the modern Age of Bronze. Man's intelligence has become attuned to the subtler vibrations of the new Age; knowledge pours in like a flood; discoveries and inventions have transformed the world as if by miracle or magic.

In the third chapter, the present writer made the following statements: "Each of the four Yugas, as described by the ancient Hindu sages, has a correspondence with one of the four powers of Maya, the darkness of Illusion that hides from man his Divine nature. Each Yuga brings to mankind in general an opportunity to control and understand one of these universal powers. The four Illusions, Abidyas, of Maya, counting from the grossest to the most subtle, are:

(1) Atomic Form, Patra or Anu, the world of gross material manifestation, wherein the One Substance appears as innumerable objects;
(2) Space, Desh, whereby the idea of division is produced in the Ever Indivisible;
(3) Time, Kal, whereby the mind conceives of change in the Ever-Unchangeable, and
(4) Vibration, Aum, the universal creative force which obscures our realization of the Ever-Uncreated. In Kali Yuga, the knowledge and power of man is confined to the world of gross matter (Bhu Loka, first sphere), and his state or natural caste is Sudra, a menial or dependent of Nature. During this Yuga, his mind is centered on the problems of material objectivity, the Abidya of Atomic Form. In Dwapara Yuga, man gains a comprehension of the electrical attributes, the finer forces and more subtle matters of creation. He now understands that all matter, atomic form, is in the last analysis nothing

but expressions of energy, vibratory force, electrical attributes. During the course of this Age of Dwapara, man is given the power to annihilate the Abidya, Illusion, of Space, and the second limitation of Maya is thereby conquered."

Time Vindicates Ancient Classifications

Has time not proved the worth of these classifications of the ancient Hindus? Has not history substantiated the accuracy of the time-periods allotted by those inspired rishis to the various World Ages as these are marked out within the 24,000-year cycle of Equinoctial Precession? Are we not now indeed in Dwapara Yuga, as testified to by the extent with which we have

(1) Comprehended the mystery of matter,
(2) Harnessed electrical energy and
(3) Conquered space?

We are no longer the Sudra dependents of Nature, nor does the institution of human slavery any longer flourish among us. Its passing had to await the coming of the mechanical and industrial revolutions which ushered in our present Age. By 1833, slavery had been abolished in all French and English colonies. Emperor Alexander II freed 23,000,000 serfs in Russia in 1861. Two years later, President Lincoln banished slavery from the New World. "If the shuttle would weave of itself," Aristotle wrote as an apology for slavery, "there would be no need of slaves." The use of machinery, with steam, compressed air and gases, and electricity as motors, has released human muscle from cruel drudgery. Simultaneously, as the physical body of man became unimportant as a source of power, the value of his mind, of his function as a thinking and reasoning individual capable of understanding and controlling machinery, increased and will continue to increase with the complexities of the Machine Age. Education of the masses has spread farther and deeper in the last two hundred years than in the previous two thousand.

The Triumph over Iron

Dwapara Yuga has been the story of man's growing power over structural materials, particularly important in the case of iron and its derivative steel. Thus have we literally triumphed over the Iron Age of Kali. "Today in the electric furnace one may see tons of

72

incandescent steel swirling about like boiling milk in a saucepan. Nothing in the previous practical advances of mankind is comparable in its consequences to the complete mastery over enormous masses of steel and iron and over their texture and quality which man has now achieved. The railways and early engines of all sorts were the mere first triumphs of the new metallurgical methods. Presently came ships of iron and steel, vast bridges, and a new way of building with steel upon a gigantic scale. In the old house or ship, matter was dominant—the material and its needs had to be slavishly obeyed; in the new, matter has been captured, changed, coerced It is in this great and growing mastery over substances, over different sorts of glass, over rocks and plasters and the like, over colors and textures, that the main triumphs of the mechanical revolution have thus far been achieved. Concurrently with this extension of mechanical possibilities the new science of electricity grew up. Suddenly came electric light and electric traction; and the transmutation of forces, the possibility of sending power, that could be changed into mechanical motion or light or heat as one chose, along a copper wire, as water is sent through a pipe, began to come through to the ideas of ordinary people. By 1909 the airplane was available for human locomotion. There had seemed to be a pause in the increase of human speed with the perfection of railways and automobile road traction, but with the flying machine came fresh reductions in the effective distance between one point of the earth's surface and another. The science of agriculture and agricultural chemistry made quite parallel advances during the 19th century. Men learned so to fertilize the soil as to produce quadruple and quintuple the crops gotten from the same area in the 17th century. There was a still more extraordinary advance in medical science; the average duration of life rose, the daily efficiency increased, the waste of life through ill health diminished. Now here altogether we have such a change in human life as to constitute a fresh phase of history."

The Future of Dwapara Yuga

We have not as yet traversed one-tenth of the Ascending Bronze Age. What modern science has already accomplished, then, is less than one-tenth of what it will accomplish by 4098 A.D. Professor Soddy, speaking of radio-activity, said, "It sounds incredible, but nevertheless it is true, that science up to the close of the 19th century had no suspicion even of the existence of the original sources of natural energy. The vista which has been opened up by these new discoveries admittedly is without parallel in the whole history of science."

Only very recently have scientists succeeded in the transmutation of elements and in the splitting of the atom. "Professor E. O. Lawrence, head of the University of California radiation laboratories," writes Harry M. Nelson, "states that when man has finally learned how to harness the power that is unleashed when an atom is smashed, he will have at his command a tremendous force, a giant that will revolutionize all present means of transportation, heat, light—perhaps our very existence. Although knowledge of the atom is confined mostly to its outer structure, recent experiments which resulted in the disintegration of the core or nucleus of the lithium atom literally open a new world to science. And judging from progress made in other branches of science as a result of experiments of a similar magnitude, it is within the realm of probabilities that the future will see an advance in the life of man such as was little dreamed of in past ages." In short, the practical use of atomic energy will render obsolete all present forms of power. "Cosmic rays," says Professor August Piccard, "may be the energy of the future, harnessed energy which will light cities, motivate industries and drive airplanes through the stratosphere at tremendous speed."

Electricity, the Unknown

As for man's present knowledge of electricity, he knows only that it exhibits, in motion, magnetic, thermal and chemical effects. He understands little of its true nature and nothing of its source, which is Chittwa, the seat of universal magnetism, and which will not be fully known until the next Age, the Silver or Treta Yuga. Though scientists from the days of Benjamin Franklin have observed that electricity appears in two ways, positive and negative, they do not properly understand its third or neutralizing manifestation. That the ancient Hindus were not mistaken in their electrical classifications is proved by the fact that it is known today that thermions or electrons emitted by a heated substance, may show an electric charge, either positive or negative, or may be uncharged (neutralized).

74

Further, modern scientists do not understand that there are five different kinds of electricities, each with three modes of manifestation. These are Pancha-Tattwa, the five root-causes of creation. The five electrical energies have their correspondence, in man's body, in his five different sensory nerve impulses, which are purely electrical in nature.5 A vast world of new interest, new research and new discoveries awaits those scientists who will study and demonstrate the grand eternal truths of universal creation laid bare so many ages ago by the ancient Hindu rishis. Dr. George W. Crile of Cleveland offers recent confirmation of very old ideas by his statement that "The human brain is governed solely by electricity, and is composed of a complex generation and distribution of power systems. It consists of no less than four quadrillion of individual dynamos, with the adrenal gland acting as the power house."

Why Ours Is the "Bronze Age"

It will be of interest here to point out the applicability of the term "Bronze Age" to our present electrical era. Bronze is an alloy of metals, chiefly copper, and it is on copper, due to its excellent conductivity and rust-resisting properties, that the electrical industry rests. Iron, ruled by Saturn, the heavy planet of limitations, was the most important metal during the two Iron Ages which preceded our present epoch. Silver and gold will doubtless be the peculiarly distinctive metals of the future Silver and Golden Ages.

Copper and bronze are under the rulership of the cooperative planet Venus, and during the centuries of the Bronze Age that lie still before us, we may reasonably expect to see the practical realization of the ideal of the Brotherhood of Man. "It doth not yet appear what we shall be" (John 3:2). The Silver and Golden Ages will be ruled, respectively, by the two luminaries, the Moon and Sun.

The power offered to the men of Dwapara Yuga, that of conquering the second Maya Illusion, of Space, has already manifested itself powerfully in the opening years of our Age, chiefly through radioactivity. We can send a radio message completely around the world in less than one-seventh of a second. To a less perfect degree, space has been mastered through the telephone, telegraph, ocean cable, television and by the airplane.

Thus far, only two of the five kinds of electricities, corresponding to sight and sound, have been developed. Three more remain for the future, when we may reach across the world to touch beloved friends and to smell and taste objects in their rooms.

The seeming limitations of space have already, in other ways, been overcome through the invention of the spectroscope. Astronomers now understand the structure and chemical composition of all the planets of our solar system and of the fixed stars, and can determine the extent and direction of motion of the solar systems beyond our own. The identity of the composition of the earth with that of the universe, the single origin, similar properties and interdependence of all the worlds of creation, have been established. Spectrum analysis has also brought to light the presence of many hitherto unsuspected elements, and science now claims the existence of ninety-two elements as the basis of cosmic creation. In the field of electro-chemistry, man has succeeded in bridging the gulf formerly supposed to exist between organic and inorganic substances; carbon, the keystone of organic compounds has been made, under electric furnace heat, to combine directly with the metals.

Other inventions of Dwapara Yuga have served the three-fold purpose of the Electrical Age; through the use of the microscope, telescope, photography and the X-Ray, man has extended the realm of his observations from the finite to the infinite, and has gained knowledge of worlds which are, respectively, otherwise too small, too remote, too transient or too dense for his sensory perception.

Chapter 11

A Widespread astrological misconception of today is the idea that the world is presently to enter, and is already feeling the vibrations of, the zodiacal Age of Aquarius. This belief is based on the fact that the Vernal Equinox, in the course of about 726 years, will have retrograded into the Sign of Aquarius. Due to lack of knowledge of the connection of the World Ages with the cycle of equinoctial precession (as explained for the first time in the western world in this series), astrologers have attempted to account of the great progress which the world has made in the last two centuries—progress due entirely to the start of the Bronze Age or Dwapara Yuga in 1698—by assuming that mankind must already be responding to the vibrations of the inventive, progressive, humanitarian Sign of Aquarius. This theory, however, is untenable. The plain fact is that the Vernal Equinox is still in the second decan of Pisces and therefore cannot be considered to be "within orbs" of an Aquarian influence. In 1698, when our present electrical Age of Dwapara began, the Vernal Equinox was falling on 13° 20' Pisces, and has today (1933) reached 13° 05' Pisces. There is no astrological justification for concluding that the great forward strides of the world in the last two hundred years could have been due to a 10° to 10° Aquarian "orb" (area of influence). An understanding of the four World Ages and their periods as related to the equinoctial cycle is the true key to world conditions of the past, present and future, and will enable astrologers to discard a number of erroneous beliefs that are current today.

Age of Leo is Approaching

A further point in this connection should be stressed. This entire series has demonstrated the truth of the ancient Hindu claim that it is the place of the Autumnal, and not the Vernal, Equinox which has significance for mankind. History has proven that the progress and decadence of the world follows, respectively, the rise and fall of the Autumnal Equinox on the zodiacal circle. It is the Autumnal Equinox which is rising at present and which is in Dwapara or the Bronze Age. A secondary Age which is being marked out by the Autumnal Equinox is the zodiacal Age of Virgo. The Vernal Equinox, on the other hand, is falling (on its Descending Arc), and is in that section of the equinoctial cycle assigned to a Golden Age, in the zodiacal Sign of Pisces. Thus it is clear that the Autumnal and not the Vernal Equinox is the true indicator of world conditions. This point is stressed here because western astrologers give first consideration to the Vernal Equinox, and call our present era the Age of Pisces. On the contrary, our zodiacal Age is that of Virgo, since the Autumnal Equinox is falling in that Sign, and in about 726 years we will enter the zodiacal Age of Leo, not Aquarius, except in a complementary sense.

It may be that the 24,000 year equinoctial cycle which we are now traversing is a female or negative cycle, and therefore the Autumnal, rather than the Vernal, Equinox is of primary importance during this period, for ancient astrological rules tell us that Libra 0° (place of the Autumnal Equinox) is the natural starting point for a female horoscope, just as Aries 0° is for a male.

Physiological Cycles

Old Hindu records tell us that a cycle of equinoctial precession is completed in 24,000 years. Western astronomers (who, unlike the Hindus, have not kept records even for one complete cycle) estimate the length of the cycle as 25,920 years, simply because the present rate of motion is about 50" yearly or one degree in 72 years (72 x 360o = 25,920). However, according to the Hindus, the rate is not constant, but varies at different stages of the cycle. The profound connection of the equinoctial cycle with human life is shown when we understand that the heartbeat of man is regulated by the equinoctial motion. The beat of a normal heart is 72 pulsations in one minute, corresponding to the 72 years which it takes the equinoxes, at present, to cover one degree of the zodiac. The equinoctial motion will increase as the Autumnal Equinox ascends on the zodiacal circle, and by the time it reaches that part of its cycle which corresponds to the Ascending Golden Age, it will be covering one degree of the zodiac in about 60 years. The heartbeat of man will then measure only 60 pulsations to the minute. As the Golden Age men will be superior to those of our present Age, it is inevitable that their heartbeats will be less per minute than the normal rate at present. It is well known that great longevity and concentration of mind are connected with slowness of heartbeat and respiration. To have conscious control over the heartbeat, to calm the

78

pulsation and to slower its pace, is, as Yogoda students know, to prolong life and rejuvenate the body cells.

Respiration and Concentration

The breath in man has a similar correspondence with the equinoctial cycle. The normal present rate of respiration in a healthy young adult is 72 breaths in four minutes or 18 breaths a minute. Golden Age men will breathe only about 60 times in four minutes. Taking fewer, longer breaths per minute is the shortest cut to concentration of mind. When one is intensely interested in any subject, one's breathing involuntarily becomes slower and slower. Consciousness is intimately connected with the breath. The faster a person breathes, the less conscious he is; his attention cannot remain fixed. Surgeons of a few hundred years ago, before anesthetics were generally used, took advantage of this knowledge, and induced unconsciousness in their patients by instructing them to breathe very fast for a few moments.

The monkey, most restless of animals, has a very rapid respiratory rate —about 32 breaths per minute. Those animals who attain great longevity have slow heartbeats and respiration. The elephant, snake and tortoise, whose life span exceeds that of man, breathe, respectively, 11, 7 and 4 times a minute.

The importance in man's life of the number 72 at the present period of the equinoctial cycle is shown in many ways —72 inches or 6 feet is the ideal height, and 72 years, corresponding closely to the "three score and ten" years of the Psalmist, is the ideal age, for the average man of the present Age. Numerous examples could be given of the correspondence between the equinoctial cycle and the rhythmic periodicity of man's physiological processes. Each man is a miniature zodiac, and faithfully reproduces in himself the movements of the solar system. "Many, O Lord my God, are the wonderful works which thou has done; if I would declare and speak of them, they are more than can be numbered." Psalm 40:5.

Starting Point of Solar System

As this series nears its conclusion, it will be of interest to examine the relationship of the equinoctial cycle with greater cycles, those which determine the duration of solar systems and universes. The ancient

Hindu rishis claimed that a new Day of Creation is ushered in with all the planets, which belong to any given solar system, placed in the same zodiacal degree. The fixed star which marked this degree would serve, throughout the entire life of the solar system, as the starting point or first degree of Aries of a fixed zodiac. The star Revati (Zeta Piscium) is considered by the Hindus to mark Aries 0° in the heavens for the present solar system.

Mr. G. E. Sutcliffe, an eminent astronomer and astrologer, in an article entitled A Day of Brahma, has proven that there is a cycle of 23,892 years (or revolutions of the Earth around the Sun) wherein three members of our solar system, Venus, Earth and Mars, return simultaneously to the first degree of the fixed zodiac. It is likely that this period of 23,892 years coincides exactly with one equinoctial cycle, and that the ancient Hindus assigned 24,000 years to the cycle, partly because of the greater convenience, for ordinary purposes, of the round numbers, and partly because the exoteric figures given out by the ancients were seldom exactly true but required esoteric interpretation or change from one scale of measurement into another. Thus, many Hindu figures which do not appear illuminative as expressions of the decimal system become clear when considered as written in duodecimal, septenary or other notations[19].

A "Day of Brahma"

If, then, we accept a period of 23,892 years as the true length of an equinoctial cycle, and bear in mind that in this period three members of our solar system return to the same zodiacal degree, we will realize that the life of our present solar system must be measured by some number that is an exact multiple of 23,892 years[20]. Sutcliffe has shown that in a period of 4,300,560 years, which exactly measures out 180 equinoctial cycles, every planetary member of our solar system returns to the first degree of Aries. An exact

---

[19] Scientists who have investigated the significance of measurements of the Great Pyramid have likewise found that the ancient architects made use of various scales, chiefly but not solely the duodecimal notation.

[20] There is a difference of only 108 years between this number and the exoteric figure of 24,000 years, and the length of the eight World Ages which are contained in one equinoctial cycle would not be appreciably shortened by taking these 108 years into consideration.

multiple of this period of Maha Yuga (4,300,560 years) will measure the life span allotted to out present solar system[21]. The Bhagavad Gita (Chapter 8, Sir Edwin Arnold's translation) sheds the following light on this point:

> If ye know Brahma's Day
> Which is a thousand Yugas;
> If ye know
> The thousand Yugas
> Making Brahma's Night,
> Then know ye Day and Night
> As He doth know!
> When that vast Dawn
> Doth break, th' Invisible
> Is brought anew into the Visible;
> When that deep Night
> Doth darken, all which is
> Fades back again to Him
> Who sent it forth .

If we consider the Maha Yuga (a thousandth part of a Kalpa) of 4,300,560 years as constituting one of the "thousand Yugas" which make a "Day of Brahma," we arrive at 4,300,560,000 years as the period of a Day of Creation or life of one solar system.3 Twice this number, of 8,601,120,000 years, will measure out the "Day and Night" of Brahma, or the period of both creation (Manvantara) and dissolution (Pralaya). Sutcliffe furnishes many intensely interesting reasons for believing that these enormous figures do accurately represent the periods of Brahma. One of his mathematical demonstrations is as follows:

"What is the numerical relation between a Day and Night of Brahma and a day and night of 24 hours? A simple multiplication will tell us this. The number of days in a sidereal year is 365.256, and 8,601,120,000 x 365.256 = 3.1416 x 1012 = n x 1012. The number 3.1416 is the relation of the diameter to the circumference of a circle and mathematicians represent it by the Greek letter n (pronounced Pi). We, therefore, see that the number of ordinary days in a Day of Brahma is n or 3.1416 multiplied by ten to the twelfth power, or multiplied by a million millions. Pi is full of occult significance; it is the symbol of the circle or cycle,

---

[21] A number of modern scientists have given their estimate of the life of the Sun as four thousand million years.

which in its turn is the symbol of Brahma, or the
Deity. When we learn, therefore, that the relationship
of an ordinary day to a Day of Brahma, or the day of
the earthly man to the Day of the Heavenly Man, can be
expressed by the figures of n, we may feel ourselves to
be on the track of the occult figures. An Age of
Brahma, we are told, consists of 100 years of Brahma so
that in figures an Age of Brahma is 314,159,000,000,000
years."

While a Day of Brahma covers the period of
existence of a solar system, an Age of Brahma measures
out the life span of an entire universe.

Thus, through the clue afforded by the period of
an equinoctial cycle, and guided by the records left us
by Hindu rishis of Golden Ages long past, we have
traced out the interrelation of the greater and lesser
cosmic cycles and measured the appointed times of suns
and universes.

Chapter 12

A study of the Equinoctial World-Age chart (diagram 1) gives us the important information that a Kali Yuga, darkest and most degenerate of the four World Ages contained in each half of the Equinoctial Cycle, is also the shortest Age. Its period of 1200 years is only half that of our present Bronze Age or Dwapara Yuga, only one-third that of the Silver Age, and only one-fourth the duration of the great Golden Age. Of a complete 24,000 year Equinoctial Cycle, only one-tenth of that time is allotted to the two Iron Ages contained in that cycle. This is indeed an inspiring reflection. However, due to the fact that the two Kali Yugas, one of the Descending and one of the Ascending Arc, merge together by combining their two periods, their united span of 2400 years occurs at one time during the world's history and leaves a longer and darker record of human ignorance and misery than would be the case if the two Kali Yugas were separated in time through the intervention of the period of one of the fairer Ages.

Pessimism Is Not Justified

Many people express pessimistic doubts that mankind is now traversing any truly ascending arc of progress which will lead ultimately to a Golden Age of universal peace, wisdom and happiness. "All history is against such an assumption," these people say, "Human misery and oppression is a fundamental condition of earth life, and have never been absent from the records of the most distant ages up until the present."

Such a gloomy view of mankind's possibilities is made possible and prevalent only because the world has but lately emerged from 2400 years of Kali Yuga domination. All our history is but Dark Age history, since the great civilizations of the world prior to the founding of Rome in 753 B.C. are known very little and misinterpreted very much. The minds of Kali Yuga men were not fit to understand the records of civilized men of higher Ages. Indeed, until the dawn of our present Bronze Age in 1698 A.D., there were, generally speaking, no scientists nor archaeologists worth the name. What slight knowledge we now have of pre-roman and pre-Grecian world conditions has all come to light in the last 200 years, since Dwapara Yuga made its appearance. We shall uncover more knowledge of antiquity as time goes on, which shall ennoble our view of the past and prove that the majority of mankind has not always been in the wretched condition of the Kali Yuga epochs (702 B.C. to 1698 A.D.).

Coming Greatness of Our Age

However, even a complete knowledge of the last Golden, Silver and Bronze Ages (11,502 to 702 B.C.) would not suffice to indicate, by analogy, to the modern world what great progress and enlightenment lie before it, because the last Golden, Silver and Bronze Ages belonged to the Descending Arc of the Equinoctial Cycle, and each year of the ancient world saw the closer arrival of a lesser Age and the loss of some part of a civilized heritage.

Whereas, the modern world, now on the Ascending Arc, has risen from the Iron Age into the greater freedom and power of the present Bronze Age, and can look forward to gradual and continual improvement and perfection for mankind for many thousands of years in the future—until the Autumnal Equinox reaches the culmination of its Ascending Arc in 12,498 A.D. At that time, no further progress will be made by the majority of mankind, and every subsequent year of that 12,000 year Arc will see the further decay of civilization.

However, Mankind shall never again fall to the depths of degradation witnessed by the last two Kali Yugas, for the next Dark Age (starting in 23,298 A.D.) will be on a higher spiral in the long, epoch-marking series of Equinoctial Cycles.

The Importance of Time

In man's slow trek toward realization of his Divinity and his consequent escape form the "wheel of life" which Ezekiel saw in his vision 2, and which the Buddha described, time is one of the essential factors. On this ground we are justified in believing that the Equinoctial Cycles follow a spiral pattern, and that each cycle sees humanity advanced beyond the previous cycle. The ancient Greeks had this thought in mind when they assigned the rulership of a Golden Age to Cronus, Saturn, planetary god of Time, since Time brings all things to perfection.

In a preceding article, it was shown that the true Age of the world at present (1933), as indicated by the position of the Autumnal Equinox on the zodiacal circle, is year 235 of Dwapara Yuga of the Ascending

Arc. Of this span, the first 200 years constituted the transition or mutation period which still retained some of the qualities of the preceding Dark Age of Iron. Only in 1898 did the true, unmodified Dwapara Yuga start.

The Coming World War

Since that year, thirty-five years have elapsed, and this span has witnessed unparalleled conditions of world unrest: the First World War of known history, the wholesale fall of kings, and the rise of dictators. Signs are not wanting that the total collapse of the whole economic, financial and social structure of the world is approaching. Thoughtful observers of the trend of events in the world today know that another World War is near at hand which will wipe out entire nations and plunge the whole earth in a sea of tears and blood.

"The next war," says Guglielmo Ferrero, the famous Italian historian, "will plunge Europe into a chaos from which it will never extricate itself. The next war is the death knell of Europe. Destruction of our western civilization." Biblical students claim that the World War which started in 1914 was the beginning of Armageddon, and that the next war will be a continuation and completion of that prophesied event.

The Old Order Must Pass

Why is it that the opening years of our great Dwapara Yuga are thus red with blood and black with destruction? It is simply because we must break with the past. Kali Yuga institutions are unable to survive the vibrations of the new Age. The children of Dwapara Yuga cannot build the fairer structure of the future civilization on the crumbling and ill-laid foundations of the Dark Age now definitely past. The power of Kali Yuga was based on the sword, and by the sword must it perish.5

The handful of people who will survive the next World War, chastened and strengthened by their sufferings, will be the parent stock of those later generations who will bring the true Bronze Age civilization into being. In the words of Isaiah, "When Thy judgments are upon the earth, the inhabitants of the world will learn righteousness." "Remembering mine affliction and my misery, and wormwood and the gall. My soul hath them still in remembrance, and is humbled in

me. This I recall to my mind, therefore have I hope."
Lamentations of Jeremiah 3:19-21.

The Bhagavad Gita gives us the following inspiring promise of Krishna, the Incarnation of God who lived at the end of the last Silver Age of the world:

When Righteousness
Declines, O Bharata! When Wickedness
Is strong, I rise, from age to age, and take
Visible shape, and move a man with men,
Succoring the good, thrusting the evil back,
And setting Virtue on her seat again.
Christ's Second Coming

The last Kali Yuga of the Descending Arc, darkest span of the whole 24,000 year Equinoctial Cycle, saw the coming of two World Saviors, Gautama the Buddha and Jesus the Christ. Jesus promised that He would come to earth again, and told his disciples of the Signs or world indications that would precede His second coming. Students of Biblical prophecy and of the prophetical measurements of the Great Pyramid (which is mentioned in Isaiah 19:19-21: "There shall be an altar to the Lord in the midst of the land of Egypt, and a pillar at the border thereof to the Lord. And it shall be for a sign and for a witness unto the Lord of hosts in the land of Egypt. And the Lord shall be known to Egypt, and the Egyptians shall know the Lord in that day") are agreed that "the time of the end" is at hand, and that the Lord shall come "in power and great glory" during the time of the next World War.

The "time of the end," so frequently mentioned in the Bible, is not the end of the world, as so many people erroneously believe, but the end of the old dispensation or order of things. The word "world" is derived from "whorl," signifying a cycle or round.

Nicholas Roerich, the great Russian traveler, painter and mystic, tells in his book, Altai-Himalaya, how widespread are the legends and manuscripts relating to Issa (Jesus) throughout all Asia. There can be little doubt that the "missing years" of Jesus' life, those years prior to the start of his ministry in Palestine, were spent in India, Tibet and other parts of Asia, and that He was known and beloved by the peoples of those countries.

Roerich has also pointed out how universal is the expectation in Asia of the near coming of a World Messiah. The Tibetans calculate the coming of "Someone of greatness" in 1936. The prophecies of Asia, Roerich says, relating to the arrival of the New Era, are: "First will begin an unprecedented war of all nations. Afterward brother shall rise against brother. Oceans of blood shall flow. Only a few years shall elapse before every one shall hear the mighty steps of the Lord of the New Era. And one can already perceive unusual manifestations and encounter unusual people. Already they open the gates of knowledge and ripened fruits are falling from the trees. .

"The new era of enlightenment is awaited. Each reaches in his own way. One nearer, one further; one beautifully, one distortedly; but all are concerned with the same predestined. It is so precious to hear and to repeat. The Motherland of Gerssar Kahn, Ladak (Tibet), knows that the time of the regeneration has come. Khotan remembers the Signs of Maitreya6 over the ancient stupa. The Kalmucks in Karashar are awaiting the coming manifestation of the Chalice of Buddha. On Altai the Oyrots renounce Shamanism and are singing new chants to the Awaited White Burkhan.6 The Messenger of the White Burkhan, Oirot, already rides throughout the world,. The Mongols await the appearance of the Ruler of the World and prepare the Dukang (temple) of Shambhala.7 On Chang-thang they extol Gessar Khan6 and whisper about the hallowed borders of Shambhala. On the Brahmaputra they know about the Ashrams of Mahatmas and remember the wonderful Azaras. The Jews await the Messiah at the Bridge. The Moslems await Muntazar.6 In Isfahan the White Horse is already saddled. The Christians of Saint Thomas await the great Advent and wear hidden signs. The Hindus know the Kalki Avatar.6 And the Chinese at New Year light the fires before the image of Gessar Khan, ruler of the World. Rigden Japo, the Ruler, is fleeting over the desert, achieving his predestined path. A blind one may ask, 'Is it so? Is there no exaggeration in it? Perhaps some fragments of survivals are taken as beliefs of the future.'

"It means that he who questions has never been in the East. If you once were upon these sites; if you traversed many thousands of miles; if you yourself have spoken to many people, then you know the reality of what is related."

Equinoctial Age Chart in Harmony with Biblical and Pyramidal Prophecy

This subject of the Lord's second coming, of Biblical prophecy and of the indications of the Great Pyramid cannot be dealt with in this article, but those who are interested will consult the works of Dr. Grattan Guinness, David Daivdson and Frederick Haberman. A very striking series of Prophecy Letters are now appearing in the magazine, "Knowing People."

It will suffice here to say that the Equinoctial World Age chart, which has been so fully dealt with in this long series of articles, is in harmony with Biblical and Pyramidal prophecies, and agrees with them in pointing out that all traces of Kali Yuga "civilization" shall soon be destroyed; that a world fairer and more righteous than our imagination can picture shall come into being as a fit symbol and manifestation of the Ascending Dwapara Yuga. "They shall beat their swords into ploughshares, and their spears into pruning hooks: nation shall not lift up sword against nation, neither shall they learn war any more." Isaiah 2:4.

The enlightenment, the achievements and the aspirations of mankind shall rise with the ascending Autumnal Equinox, in conformance with God's great plan for His children of earth. He has written His message in the stars, that all who will, may read. "The heavens declare the glory of God, and the firmament showeth His handiwork. Day unto day uttereth speech, and night unto night showeth knowledge. There is no speech nor language where their voice (influence) is not heard. Their line (vibration) is gone out through all the earth, and their words to the end of the world." Psalms 19:1-4.

Chapter 13

Lemuria and Atlantis

A Striking proof of the truth of the cyclic nature of man's progress and decadence, and of the presence on this earth of high civilizations tens of thousands of years ago, has been offered during recent years by geological and archaeological evidence of the existence and culture of the sunken continents of Lemuria and Atlantis. Colonel James Churchward's three scholarly books on Mu (Lemuria) point out that Lemuria was the "mother of the world" and that her civilization was vastly more ancient than that of Atlantis. The latter was colonized by emigrants from Lemuria.

Churchward advances many interesting reasons to support his belief that Lemurians brought their civilization to ancient Egypt, Greece and other parts of the world. The Egyptian Book of the Dead is a sacred memorial to the Lemurian forefathers of the Egyptians who perished when Mu sank under the blue waters of the Pacific. Churchward translates the Egyptian hieroglyphic name of this book, Per-m-hru, as "Mu has gone forth from the day." The relation of the ancient Greeks to Mu is shown forth by the construction of the Greek alphabet which, as Churchward proves, "is composed of Cara-Maya vocables forming an epic that relates the destruction of Mu."

This theory, that colonists from Lemuria, and later from Atlantis, spread their civilization all over the ancient world, is not accepted by many scholars, but it must be admitted that it is the only explanation that satisfactorily accounts for the otherwise puzzling similarities to be found in the ancient architecture, art, language, religion, traditions and customs of widely separated lands, such as Central America and Mexico on one side of the world, and Egypt and Babylonia on the other.

Plato's Writings on Atlantis

The story of Atlantis is better known, because more recent, than that of Lemuria. The famous Republic of Plato was largely inspired by Greek traditions founded on memories of the great civilization of Atlantis, and in two other books, the Timaeus and Critias, Plato gives vivid descriptions of the lost continent and its people. Other ancient Greeks wrote about Atlantis a the "blessed," "happy" or "fortunate" land, the Edenic garden of the world in a long-past Golden Age, remote even to the Greeks of Plato's time. Roman writers of the same period referred to the vast sea between Europe and America as Maris Atlantici, the Atlantic Ocean, thus indicating their belief that these waters covered the Atlantean continent.

The Atlanteans are described by Plato and others as having been in possession of marvelous scientific knowledge and power. Particularly notable was their conquest of space by the use of airplanes1 and through television. Churchward believes that the Lemurians and Atlanteans spread the knowledge of aerial travel over all the ancient world. He writes, in his fascinating book, The Children of Mu:

Ancient Knowledge of Airplanes

"These are the most detailed accounts I have found about the airships of the Hindus 15,000 to 20,000 years ago, except one which is a drawing and instructions for the construction of the airship and her machinery, power, engine, etc. The power is taken from the atmosphere in a very simple inexpensive manner. The engine is somewhat like our present-day turbine in that it works from one chamber into another until finally exhausted. When the engine is once started it never stops until turned off. It will continue on if allowed to do so until the bearings are worn out. These ships could keep circling around the earth without ever once coming down until the machinery wore out. The power is unlimited, or rather limited only by what metals will stand. I find various flights spoken of which according to our maps would run from 1000 to 3000 miles. All records relating to these airships distinctly state that they were self-moving, they propelled themselves; in other words, they generated their own power as they flew along. They were independent of all fuel. It seems to me, in the face of this, and with all our boasting, we are about 15,000 to 20,000 years behind the times. There are many Chinese records of about the same date regarding these ancient flying machines." It is noteworthy that recent excavations in Crete have brought to light records which mention Cretan airplanes.

King Chronos of Atlantis

Though Plato's account of Atlantis met with slight credence from scientists up until recent times, the

90

discoveries of Dr. Henry Schliemann, eminent archeologist, have placed the existence of that land beyond doubt. "When in 1873," writes Dr. Schliemann, "I made the excavation of the ruins of Troy at Hissarlik and discovered in the second city the famous treasures of Priam, I found among that treasure a peculiar bronze vase of great size. Engraved in Phoenician hieroglyphics with a sentence which reads: 'From the King Chronos of Atlantis'. Among a collection of objects from Tiahaunaco, South America, is another vase identically the same as I found among the treasures of Priam."

The significance of the Phoenician hieroglyphics is explained by Professor Nicola Russo, in The Atlantis Quarterly: "The Phoenician alphabet, which is the first of all the European alphabets, is derived from the Atlantean alphabet, which was taught to the Maya of Central America. Atlantis was the home of the Aryan or indo-European, and of the Semitic, not excluding the Turanian, peoples. The male and female divinities of the ancient Greeks, of the Phoenicians, of the Indians, and of the Scandinavians, were kings, queens and heroes of Atlantis, and the acts of heroism which mythology attributes to them are none other than a confused record of historical happenings. Atlantis perished in a terrible convulsion of nature, in which the entire island was submerged, with the loss of all the population. Those few who had time to escape from the general disaster on boats and on rafts carried the account of the event to the people who were in the East and West —a tradition that has come down to our days with the legend of the universal Deluge. That Atlantis before the time of Plato was known in sacred traditions and legends is proved by the fact that Homer and Hesiod were already acquainted with the legend of Atlas, condemned by Jove to bear the heavens on his shoulders. Herodotus also, in the fourth book of his History, mentions the Atlanteans, and Diodorus, in his Library of History, tells of the Atlanteans, a people more civilized than the people of these countries, and inhabiting a rich land containing many cities."

Lewis Spence, the learned scientist whose researches have thrown important light on the vanished civilizations of Atlantis and Lemuria, points out that Suidas claimed that both Homer and Hesiod were Atlanteans. In the Homeric epics, the blind bard "sings of his country, the country of the gods, Atlantis".

The vases found by Schliemann establishes the fact that there was a King Chronos of Atlantis, and in this connection it is of interest to note that the ancient Greeks preserved traditions of their Golden Age, which they made coincident with the reign of a King Chronos, who may well have been the ruler over the Atlantean forefathers of the Greeks.

A group of survivors of the Atlantean cataclysm settled in northwest Africa, and were known as "Atlanteans" to Greek and Roman writers, who named the Atlas Mountains, in that region, in their honor —Atlas being the Latin singular form of Atlantes.

Scientists of the Carnegie Institution, recently excavating at Chichen Itza, in Yucatan, found, among the imposing ruins of the Pyramid of the Warriors, a Temple dedicated to the Atlanteans.

Island Remnants of Atlantis

The Antilles group of islands in the West Indies, and the Azore and Canary Islands off the northwest coast of Africa, are believed by competent scholars to constitute veritable remnants of Atlantis, and to indicate roughly the extent of her western and eastern boundaries. All these island groups are situated on an ocean ridge which is subject to great earthquakes, and this region, according to Scott-Elliott, "has been the scene of volcanic disturbance on a gigantic scale, and that within a quite measurable period of geologic time."

An article in The Atlantis Quarterly for September 1932 refers to a recent discovery by the archeologist, Nicolas de Ascanio, on Teneriffe, largest island of the Canaries, of vases and pottery "of exquisite proportions and workmanship. M. de Ascanio does not hesitate to assert that the pottery and mortar in question are, 'with the exception of arms, the most ancient products of human industry actually known'. That we are here in the presence of remains of an advanced civilization that existed long before the present race of aboriginals inhabited the islands cannot be doubted. The conclusion that the beautiful examples of ceramic art under discussion are veritable relics of Atlantean craftsmanship is, we think, established, and constitutes one of the most remarkable corroborations of Plato's history of Atlantis."

Professor Russo, in an article in the same issue of the magazine above referred to, stresses the importance of the results of a scientific expedition in the ship Meteor around the Azores. "The mythical island, which has been the object of so many studious investigations, according to the testimony of a recent German scientific expedition, must have been located where the Azores now lie, and the peaks of the Azores must be the tops of the mountains of the submerged Atlantis. The contour of the upper submarine plane of the Azores sounded by the ship Meteor is indicated to us exactly by the situation and the conformation of Atlantis, in accordance with what is left to us in their writings by Plato and the geographers of antiquity. This is the reason why the learned Germans maintain the submersion of Atlantis must be calculated as 9,500 years B.C., a period during which the earth penetrated into the mooned ray of action. Under the magnetic influence of this satellite, the waters of the ocean rose to the point of overwhelming Atlantis, so that only the tops of the highest mountains remained. The communications of these scholars come opportunely to throw light upon the darkness of so many mysteries that enwrap the Edenic Island, they serve as a link connecting Egypt and South America, and exhibit the similarities of the characteristics of their civilizations."

Submergence About 9,500 B.C.

Lewis Spence believes that continental Atlantis was destroyed at the end of the Tertiary period (Miocene times), leaving two large islands. One of these, the largest, was the only Atlantis with which the ancient Greek and Roman writers were acquainted. Most of this island was finally submerged by a cataclysm of nature at a date which geological, historical and traditional evidence agrees on as about 9,500 B.C.

Plutarch tells us that Solon, the Athenian law-giver and ancestor of Plato, visited Egypt in 600 B.C., and that "Souchis, a priest of Sais, and Psenophis, a priest of Heliopolis, told him that 9000 years before, the relations of the Egyptians with the lands of the west had been interrupted because of the mud which had made the sea impassable after the destruction of Atlantis."

"When Atlantis was first submerged," Churchward writes, "she only went down deep enough to be awash at low tide so that at low tide mud banks appeared with masses of seaweed which made the northern Atlantic impassable to shipping." This was the real reason why the ancient Greeks never ventured to sail beyond the Pillars of Hercules (Strait of Gibraltar). Later on, Atlantis sank to her present depth, and ships could move freely over her burial place.

Some ancient writers refer to Atlantis as Poseidon. "An Egyptian papyrus states that Poseidon was the first king of Atlantis and that he was followed by a long line of Poseidons, thus forming a Poseidon Dynasty" (Churchward).

The Platonic story tells us that "Atlantis was the center of civilization and conquered the whole world." Dr. Schliemann makes the following observations on the connection of Egypt with Atlantis: "In the Museum at St. Petersburg, Russia, there is a papyrus roll, one of the oldest known. It was written in the reign of Pharaoh Sent of the Second Dynasty. The papyrus relates that 'Pharaoh Sent out an expedition to the west in search of traces of the Land of Atlantis from whence, 3350 years before, the ancestors of the Egyptians arrived, carrying with themselves all of the wisdom of their native land. The expedition returned after five years with the report that they had found neither people nor objects which could give them a clue to the vanished land.' Another papyrus in the same Museum by Manetho, the Egyptian priest-historian, gives a reference of a period of 13,900 years as the reign of the Sages of Atlantis. This papyrus places the height of the civilization of Atlantis at the very beginning of Egyptian history, approximately 16,000 years ago."

Spence tells us that the modern Basques who dwell in the Pyrenees "have not hesitated to announce themselves as the last branch of the Atlantean race — and perhaps not without reason, for it is within the bounds of probability that they are descended from the Cro-Magnon race which would seem to have reached Iberian soil from an oceanic area."

Etymology of "Atlantic"

Brasseur de Bourbourg, a writer of the last century, traced the etymology of the word Atlantic in the following way: The words Atlas and Atlantic have no

94

satisfactory etymology in any language known to Europe. They are not Greek, and cannot be referred to any known language of the Old World. But in the Nahu-atlan language (peculiar to the Toltec tribes of ancient Mexico) we find immediately the radical a, atl, which signifies water, war, and the top of the head. From this comes a series of words, such as atlan, or the border of or amid the water; from which we have the adjective Atlantic. A city named Atlan existed when the continent was discovered by Columbus, at the entrance of the Gulf of Uraha." Another city, existing today, with a similar name, is Mazatlan, on the west coast of Mexico. It is an interesting fact, mentioned by some of the early European voyagers to this country, that certain Indian tribes called the whole continent of America by the name of Atlanta. The Nahuatlan language, as its name implies, is similar to and derived from the Atlantean language, for the ancient Maya and Toltec civilizations, so similar in many ways to that of Egypt, were brought to Mexico and Yucatan from Atlantis, who in turn was a colony of Lemuria, "mother of the world."

The subject of Atlantis, her magnificent civilization and her dramatic end, has exercised a fascination for modern as well as ancient authors. Besides the scholarly works, published in the last fifty years, by such scientists as Ignatius Donally, Schliemann, Spence, Russo and Churchward, many imaginative novels have been written around Atlantis. "A Dweller on Two Planets" by Phylos, is stimulating reading. A romance, "L'Atlantide," by Benoit, has recently been produced in France as a motion picture. "The Coming Race" by Bulwer-Lytton, very popular with a previous generation, was based on Atlantean traditions. Recently two French writers have compiled a Bibliography of Atlantis, giving over 1700 references. "Societies for Atlantean Studies" now exist in France, Italy and other European lands.

Francis Bacon, "father of experimental philosophy," wrote a stirring book in the 17th century, outlining a great plan for the development of scientific learning which was to remold the institutions of the world on a fairer basis. The founding of the Royal Society of London in 1662 was a direct result of Lord Bacon's inspiring work, which was named "The New Atlantis".

Kriya Yoga Line of Gurus

It was said that Yogananda cast a wide net, using modern marketing and publicity to attract as many people as possible. He is certainly the most well known of all the teachers in the Kriya Yoga Line of Gurus. The lists below show the relationships from Lahiri to Sri Yukteswar to Yogananda to those direct disciples still living such as Swami Kriyananda and Roy E. Davis.

Essentially only one long branch and a few leaves are shown from a mighty trunk with many branches. The author does not intend to promote one branch or leaf over any other, merely showing the relationships to each other. The apt researcher will find much discussion between the branches over the merits of American style marketing and publicity and the simplifications of the practices and techniques for a broad audience. Fame and renown have certain monetary benefits and there is a certain amount of jostling for being the "most authentic". Discrimination is left to the reader.

What seems clear to the author is that each guru showed the divine light according to the lens of his nature, for example, in devotion with Yogananda and Satyananda and in a dryer, more scientific manner for Sri Yukteswar and Dhirananda.

Mahavatar Babaji guru of:
• Swami Lahiri Mahasaya

Swami Lahiri Mahasaya guru of:
• Panchanan Bhattacharya (founded Aryya Mission Institution)
• Swami Mahabir
• Swami Kebalananda
• Swami Pranabananda
• Brahmachari Kesavananda
• Tinkori Lahiri
• Dukori Lahiri
• Swami Sri Yukteswar (founded Sadhu Sabha and Satsanga Sabha)
• Brajalal Adhikari
• Prasad Das Goswami
• Kali Kumar Banerjee

- Kesav Chandra Banerjee
- Ram Dayal Mazumder
- Hari Narayan Palodhi
- Bhupendranath Sanyal
- Brajalal Adhikari
- Joyram Bhattacharya
- Ramarupa Bhattacharya
- Kailash Chandra Benerjee
- Kanti Acharya

Swami Sri Yukteswar guru of:
- Motilal Mukherjee
- Swami Satyananda (initiated by Kebalananda, faithful to the end)
- Swami (later) Paramhansa Yogananda
- (founded YSS Inc., Ranchi School and SRF Inc.)
- Swami Bhabananda Giri
- Swami Paramananda
- Swami Narayana
- Amulya Charan Santra
- Bijoy Kumar Chatterjee
- Bipin Chandra Bhumia
- Swami Dhirananda (initiated by Kebalananda, left SRF Inc.)
- Sri Sailendra Bejoy Das Gupta
- Golakananda Giri
- Dasarathi Chatterjee

Paramhansa Yogananda guru of:
- Swami Atmananda
- Swami Sevananda
- Swami Sadananda
- Swami Binayananda
- Swami Bidyananda
- Swami Satchidananda
- Swami Premananda
  (left SRF Inc., founded Self-Revelation Church)
- Swami Kriyananda (left SRF Inc., founded Ananda)
- Swami Hariharananda (founded Kriya Yoga Institute)

Yogananda explicitly said there would be no gurus in the SRF Inc./YSS Inc. line and that the writings would be the guru, when he was gone. SRF Inc. and YSS

Inc. provide heavily censored[22] versions of his books. Original works can be found from Ananda[23] and lessons from the Dallas Amrita Foundation[24]. Further material can be found via Yoga Niketan[25].

Some notable Yogananda disciples and their dates of first meeting him are:

- 1920 Boston, Dr. Lewis - First US Devotee
- 1924 San Francisco, Tara Mata – Yogananda's editor
- 1930 Detroit, Yogacharya Oliver Black (left SRF Inc., founded Song of the morning) - Second most advanced male devotee
- 1931 Salt Lake City, Daya Mata, her sister, Ananda Mata, mother and brother, Richard Wright – have controlled SRF Inc. since 1955
- 1932 Kansas, Rajarsi Janakananda - Most advanced male devotee, President after Yogananda's death, until his own in 1955
- 1947 Los Angeles, Norman Paulsen (left SRF Inc., founded Sunburst)
- 1948 Los Angeles, Swami Kriyananda (left SRF Inc., founded Ananda)
- 1949 Los Angeles, Roy Davis (left SRF Inc., founded Center for Spiritual Awareness)

A complete list would be huge; the diaspora of SRF Inc. ex Nuns and ex Monks has grown by over fifty in just the last ten years. Many of the ex Monastics in turn form organizations and so on. One of the earliest spin offs was by Hamid Bey[26]. Either directly, through his books, or through followers, Yogananda (and his gurus)'s influence on the West has been huge.

Even such seemingly mainstream authors as JD Salinger were influenced by the teachings. The reader is cautioned against assuming that an organizational role or (more commonly in the US) ex-organizational role is a guarantee of enlightenment.

---

[22] yoganandarediscovered.org/jaitruth/changes.html
[23] ananda.org
[24] amrita.com
[25] yoganiketan.net
[26] coptic-sun.org

Major Kriya Yoga Organizations in the United States

Ananda	ananda.org
Center for Spiritual Awareness	csa-davis.org
Kriya Yoga Institute	kriya.org
Self-Revelation church	self-revelationchurch.org
Song of the Morning	goldenlotus.org
SRF Inc.	srf-yogananda.org
Sunburst	sunburstonline.org

About this book

"Astrological World Cycles, Original First Edition, Copyright 1933 by Tara Mata (Laurie Pratt)" is the 75th anniversary edition of the tour de force series of articles in Paramhansa Yogananda's East-West magazine demonstrating the connection of the astronomical phenomenon known as the precession of the equinoxes with the great cycles of world history, astrology and ancient Hindu Scripture.

Tara was an astrologer, direct disciple and chief editor of the Indian yogi Paramhansa Yogananda, author of the 1946 spiritual classic "Autobiography of a Yogi". Tara's articles were based on the work of Yogananda's guru, Sri Yukteswar. At the time of publication in the early 30s, yoga and Yogananda were relatively unknown. Tara helped build Yogananda's organization, SRF Inc., and indirectly inspired the creation of its largest spin-off, Ananda, formed by its vice-president Swami Kriyananda. Over the past decades interest has dramatically increased as many of the guru's predictions have been proven.

Tara came from an intellectually brilliant family, related to both Joseph Smith, Jr., the founder of The Church of Jesus Christ of the Latter Day Saints (LDS or Mormons) and Mitt Romney, presidential candidate. Her grandfather, Orson Pratt, was the editor for Joseph Smith, Jr. Yogananda said of Tara: "It is not necessary for her to meditate in this life. By editing my writings, and because she came here a highly realized soul, she does not require this. I have already set her place for her in heaven."

CPSIA information can be obtained
at www.ICGtesting.com
Printed in the USA
LVOW03s1148161215
466840LV00004B/579/P